The Hunt/Speedball
Calligraphy Workbook...

An Italic Notebook

by Abraham Lincoln

With easy to follow lessons
prepared in simple form
for students of all ages

Published by Calligrafree the calligraphy company

Copy number

First Edition, Revised

Seventeenth Printing
March 1986

For my wife Pat; and my children; Angela, Chris, Melinda, Becky and Melissa.

ISBN 0-942032-00-4

Library of Congress Catalog Card No.: 78-56645

Contents

Contents	iii, iv, v, vi
Acknowledgements	vii
Foreword	x
Preface	viii - ix
For Study	1 - 2.
Cursive Italic	3 - 4.
Pen to Paper	5.
Stay on the 45°	6, 7, 8
Letter slant	9.
Things to look for	10 - 11.
Part 1 - Italic	12.
Assignment: a, g, d, q. b, p.	13 - 14.
Assignment: h, n, m, u, y, r.	15 - 16.
Assignment: i, l, j.	17.
Assignment: k, e, v, w, f, t.	18 - 19 - 20.
Assignment: o, s, x, z.	20 - 21.
Assignment: b, d, h, k, l, q.	22.
Assignment: c, tt, ff, st, ct, pp.	23.
Assignment: ft, ab, gd, oc, ke, Rb.	24.
Assignment: 12, 80, 34, 56, 79, &	25.

Part 2 - Cursive Italic 26.
Assignment: a, b, c, d, e, f. 27.
Assignment: i, j, g, h, k, l. 28.
Assignment: m, n, m, n, o, p. 29.
Assignment: q, r, s, t, u, v. 30.
Assignment: w, y, x, y, z, tt. 31.
A final word about cursive italic 32.
Part 3 - Capitals 33.
Assignment: Aa, Bb, Cc, Dd, Ee, Ff, Gg, Hh. 34.
Assignment: Ii, Jj, Kk, Ll, Mm, Nn, Oo, Pp, Qq. 35.
Assignment: Rr, Ss, Tt, Uu, Vv, Ww, Xx, Yy, Zz. 36.
Assignment: A, B, C, D, E, F. 37.
Assignment: G, H, I & J, K, L, M. 38.
Assignment: N, O, P, R, S, T. 39.
Assignment: U, V, W, X, Y, Z. 40.
Flourishes 41-42.
Assignment: Write a row of names 43.
Miscellaneous information 44.
Part 4 - Study & Experiments 45.
Writing up against the line 46.
Letter format 47-49.
Note format 50.

Invitation format 51.
Unexpectedly 52.
Paper & Printers 53.
Printing Tips 54-55.
Inks 56.
Questions & Answers 57-59.
Examples of Italic by master & student 60-65.
Part 5 - Bookhand 66.
Assignment: ı, a, b, c, d, e. 67.
Assignment: f, g, h, i, j, k. 68.
Assignment: l, m, n, o, p, q. 69.
Assignment: r, s, st, t, u, v. 70.
Assignment: w, x, y, z, ct, st. 71.
Assignment: b, d, h, k, l, p. 72.
Part 6 - Rustic 73.
Assignment: A, B, C, D, E 74.
Assignment: F, G, H, I, J. 75.
Assignment: K, L, M, N, O. 76.
Assignment: P, Q, R, S, T, V. 77.
Assignment: W, X, Y, Z, P. 78.
Part 7 - Chancery Italic, Carolingian & Uncial 79.
For study or practice 80-85.

Part 8 - *Quills* 86.
Brief account of use 87.
How to cut and temper quills 88-91.
Part 9 - *Miscellaneous*
Assignment sheet blank 92.
Some essential things to look for 93.
Supplies you'll want to order from catalog 94.
So you want to teach 95.
A Final Word 96.

to all of the people who are involved, with one another, in the promotion of improved handwriting and calligraphy and, a special "thank you" to the people listed below, for individual calligraphy, and handwritten contributions:

Alfred Fairbank · 1931 Woodside Writing Card · published by Dryad Press
James Hayes · Raymond DaBoll · Martin Jackson · Irene Alexander · Arlyne Gonczewski · Ann Kette · Buddy Blackwell · Marion Andrews · Jerry Barber · Marvin Coleman · Esmé Davis · Calligrafree · and to those I have omitted; all of my students, and to my family.

"Verba volant, scripta manent" — Spoken words fly away, but written words remain.

Preface

There are many books about calligraphy and Italic Handwriting. Some are very good and others are very poor. This is a workbook and calligraphy workbooks are very rare.

This workbook is as simple as I could write it. The format has been tested more than four years with outstanding results. Thousands of Students, from eight to eighty, have used this format in my two other books. It works.

Instructions in the book are clear and to the point. If the workbook is used in the classroom, a complete set of Lesson Plans is available, with behavorial objectives, lists of materials, cited references and suggested tests. Regular notebook paper can be used for practice work.

Each letter form in the workbook is an abstract conception of an imaginary ideal form. Neither the writing nor the models are perfect since perfect letter forms are not known to exist. Models are the renderings of forms many centuries old. Historic forms are held in high regard because some have survived the test of time and careless abandon. We need to study them and learn to write them well.

In my opinion, this book is your best answer to many handwriting problems. It will provide you with an excellent opportunity to learn about calligraphy in a short period of time with a minimum investment.

Abraham Lincoln
June 1978

Foreword

Alphabets are very old and delicate. Over many years, people have used available alphabets to communicate. Most have done so without wrecking legibility by destroying essential forms. Many more have destroyed legibility, surrendering their identity to machines. They have lost their ability to "write" their own names. Instead of writing their name, they are reduced to the job of SIGNING their name. An "X" being an uneducated individual's "signature", & an abstract scrawl the "modern equivalent". When we realize that, written records have made the words and laws of God available as well as the wisdom of all ages, we will begin to write each letter of the alphabet with great care. Until then, be content to write, in this space age, with this alphabet, which has survived the test of centuries. And be thankful that you can still read and write. Some institutions have said that writing is obsolete and that we will be a talking & listening people. God forbid!

For Study

A student should study all of the material with care. Try to retain all of it. Be patient & practice as you go through the book. Use wide ruled notebook paper for practice work.

Be a calm and quiet student & you'll learn more.

Italic terms

A a d g st Q

Capital letters are called "Majuscules" A printer would call them "upper case." The word "capital" is commonly used by scribes. A small letter is called a "Minuscule." Printers say "lower case." Small letters, minuscules, were once majuscules. Call them "small letters" and everyone knows what you mean. Parts of some small letters are called "Ascenders" & other parts on others are called "Descenders". If the part is on top it is an "Ascender" and on the bottom, it is a descender. The central portion of a letter is its "Main Body." All minuscules are to use three lines (guide lines) of writing space. A main body fits between spaces for ascenders and descenders Each space is assigned to the specific letter or a portion of it. Some letters are tied together in standard "Ligatures." A "Flourish" extends a part of a letter.

Ascenders
Main body elf
Descenders

Cursive Italic

Find a comfortable chair and writing surface. Place your writing paper and pens in any normal as well as comfortable position upon the writing surface. Look at your pen point. It isn't pointed but resembles a chisel. We call it a square cut, pen nib.

A typical pointed pen will only leave a single weight line — just like a ball pointed pen. Chisel or square cut pen nibs automatically leave a line which is shaded; or, thick and thin. All you need to do, is guide the pen so the thicks and thins are in the right places.

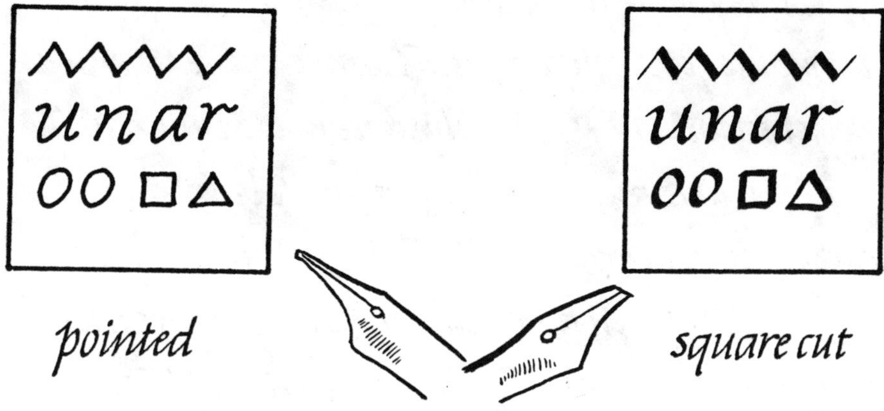

Our alphabets were developed by right-handed scribes. Left-handed people may find it awkward to duplicate all of the letters. The oblique cut pen is used by left-handed scribes. The paper can be canted so that the left side is higher-up than the right side.

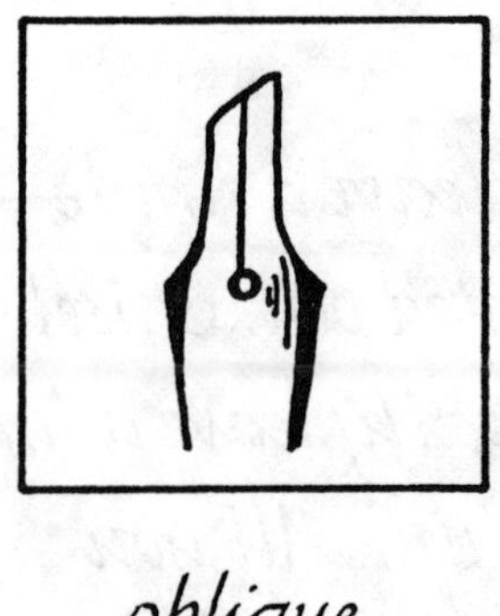

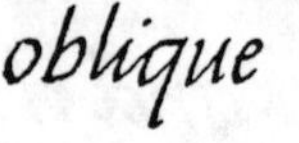

oblique

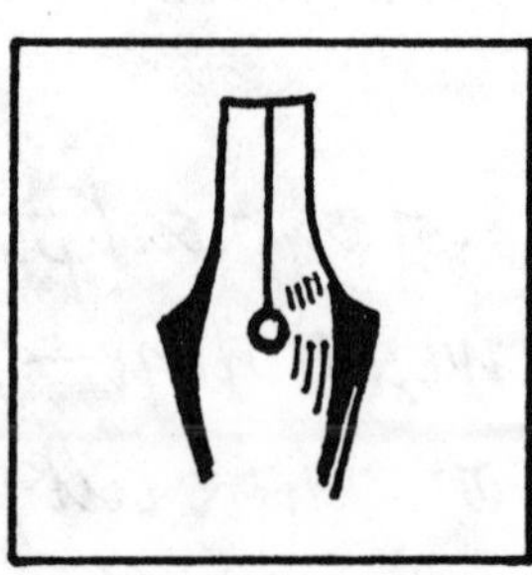

square

Good teachers want to help and encourage students to become good penpersons. A competent teacher is also a good scribe. W. R. Lethaby once wrote that handwriting "... is an amazing art really - to be improved rather than degraded." Teachers should know the difference between awkwardness and creativeness and recognize them early. Do not be too critical. Encourage.

Pen to Paper

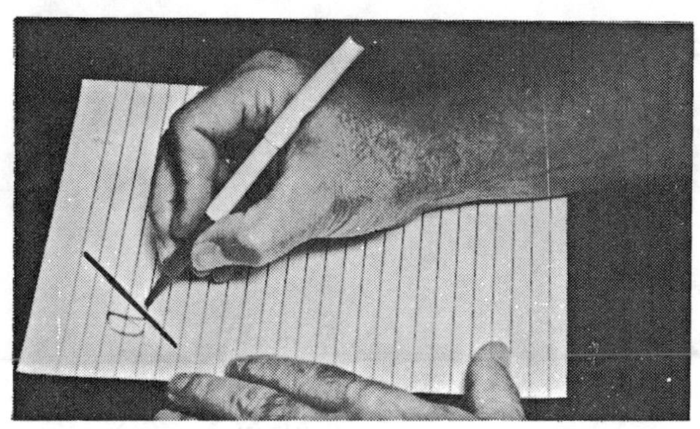

Perhaps the most important thing to remember about italic is the way the pen is held on the paper. It must be on forty-five degrees.

The flat, or chisel edge, is held on 45° with respect to lines, for writing, on the paper. Hold the pen on 45° and guide it through the letters form. The pen will automatically produce thicks & thins in the proper places, provided you've made the form properly.

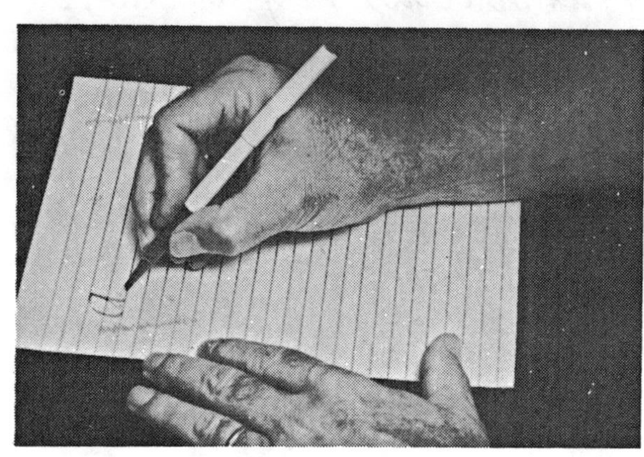

Paper can be held straight or canted. I much prefer it to be canted, but would like students to have it straight as shown.

Stay on the 45°

pen nib angle. Eventually it will be a normal & routine thing you'll do when writing italic.

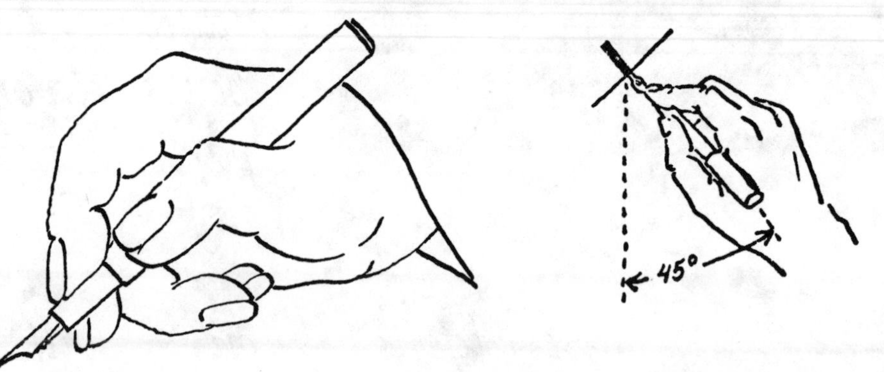

A square cut pen nib can be held in any way as long as it is aimed in such a way so that it is aligned along a 45° diagonal line.

When properly aligned the pen nib would make its thinnest line in a box from top right corner to bottom left corner. It would make its thickest line to each of the opposite corners, as shown here.

Therefore, a good alignment check is the perfect, thick and thin x.

If you were to place your pen on the paper, so its square edge is parallel with the lines on the paper, you would be ready to write Uncials but not Italic. The thicks and thins of each letter would occur at the wrong places for Italic.

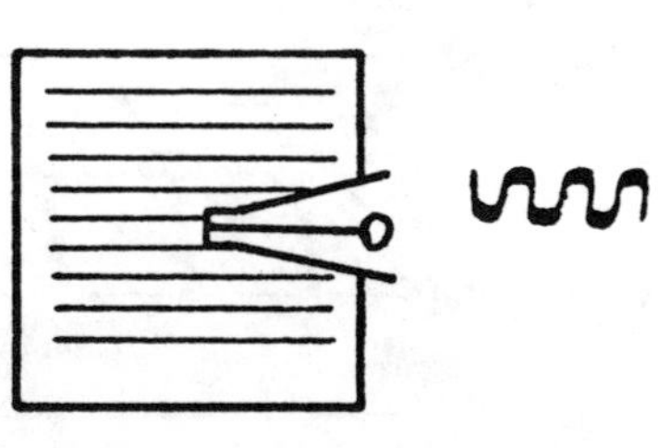

When held vertically the pen is ready, almost, to write Rustic, but not Italic. In this situation, thicks and thins occur at the exact opposite places as they do for Uncials, above.

We compromise and hold the pen on 45°. Thicks and thins now occur on a 45° diagonal line. So, always check the pen position, & a square box is provided for that purpose on many assignments. Its there to help you, so please use it. Line your pen nib up on the line already in the square box.

Forty-five degrees is the correct pen nib angle. It is used in italic and other styles.

Practice these movements:

un

mu

um

Best

letter slant 7 -10°

italic

pen angle 45°

7° to 10° is the best slant to write italic on. Seven to ten degrees. Strive for this angle.

italic

0° or vertical italic is preferred by some scribes. Zero to ten degrees is acceptable.

italic

15° to 17° is the critical area. It is common in rapid handwriting. Fifteen to seventeen degrees would be the limit. Just 1° to 2° beyond the limit and legibility will begin to disappear. Although these examples are legible, you'll have to accept what is said until you are able to prove it to yourself. At 22°, italic form can be destroyed. I'm not able to help those who might insist upon using a backhand italic.

italic

italic

italic

Things to Look for

a

a, d, g, q, c, b & p: have flat tops, or, the b & p have flat bottoms. The triangle should not exceed ½ the vertical stroke.

flat

flat

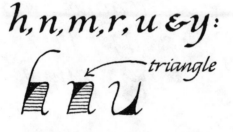

All outside curves on main body are gentle. Make the counters (shaded areas) equal.

h

h, n, m, r, u & y: all of these are very much alike. The same triangle rule is applicable and try to make all counters similar.

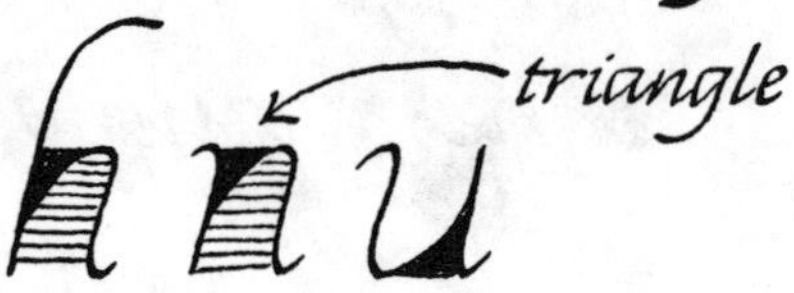

triangle

k

ke

k & e: the "loop" or "bowl" are not exactly the same.

s

The s shown at left is not good, but the one at the right, made in 3 strokes, is better. Do you see why?

s

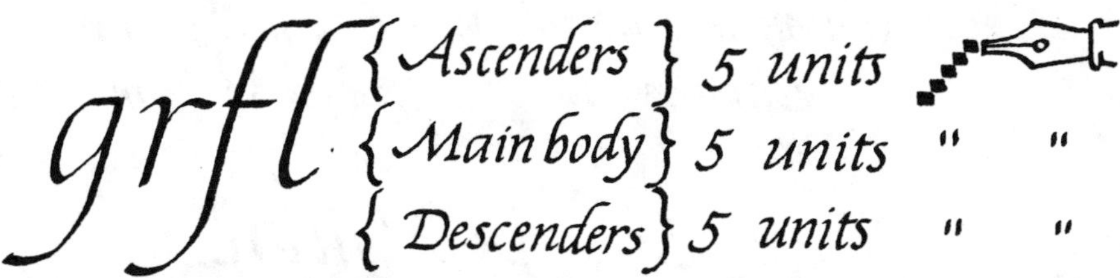

Notice that the pen nib (at top right) made the required "units" but they do not quite fill-up the space — thus the letters g, r, f, l, seem to be tall and too skinny. We must use a nib, on this paper, which is a wee bit wider.

In this situation, the pen nib is a wee bit too large to use on this ruled notebook paper.

Ordinarily, you can rule your own, like these, lines to fit your nibs; or buy them.

} this pen was very close.

grfl

This pen was a tiny bit too small. But in writing a note a little bit won't be noticed.

Nanbncndnenfngnhninjnknlnmnnnonpnqnrnsnt nunvnwnxnyn&nz Smile – it's monday.....

Keep even pressure on nib.

A pessimist is one who feels bad when he feels good for fear he'll feel worse when he feels better.

I feel more like I do now than I did awhile ago.

· ANONYMOUS ·

Don't think of retiring from the world until the world will be sorry that you retire. I hate a fellow whom pride or cowardice or laziness drive into a corner, and does nothing when he is there but sit and and growl. Let him come out as I do, and bark.

Samuel Johnson

The reward of a thing well done is to have done it.

RALPH WALDO EMERSON

Mar·Co 6·27·77

-353-

50% reduction

This is page 353 of "365 Days With A Broad Pen" – It is a page of practice writing by Marvin Coleman. He did one page every day for one year for practice purposes only.

PART I

Be a patient person from this page on. Practice all of the time if you can. Do not be content with your best efforts but strive to make your best even better. Learn to look at a letter and see its secret parts; and study the writing of the masters when you can. Remember, "verba volant, scripta manent."

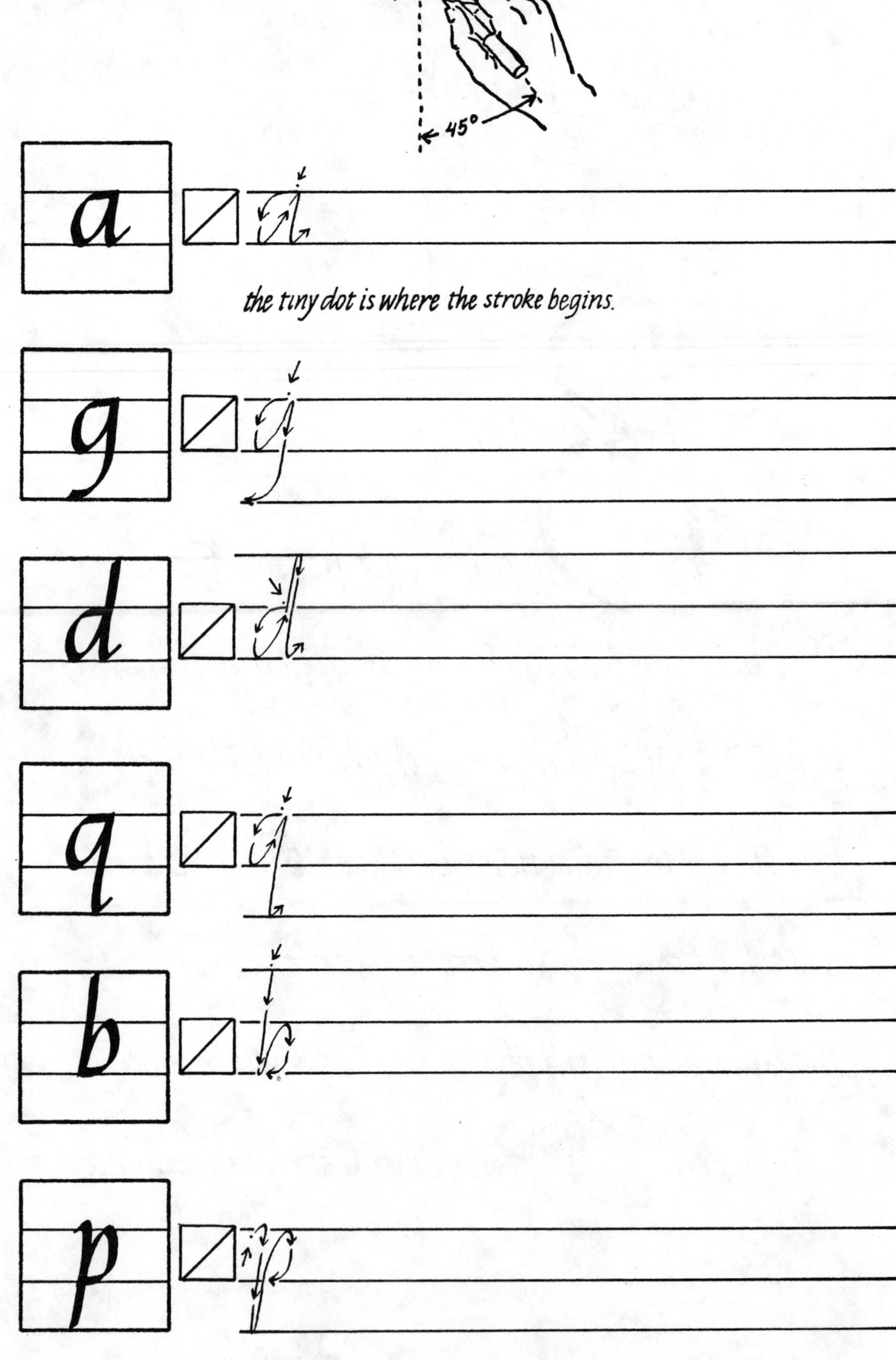

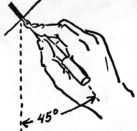

Line your pen up on 45° diagonal line and write the forms on the lines as shown in the examples.

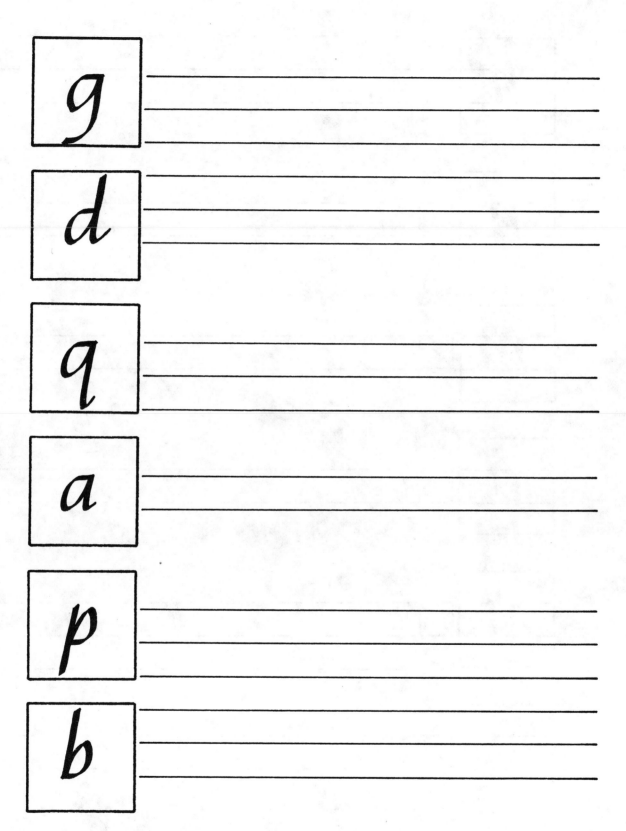

g

d

q

a

p

b

Write one line at a time and try to duplicate the examples

Line your pen up on the 45° diagonal line and write the forms on the lines as shown by the examples.

h

n

m

u

y

r

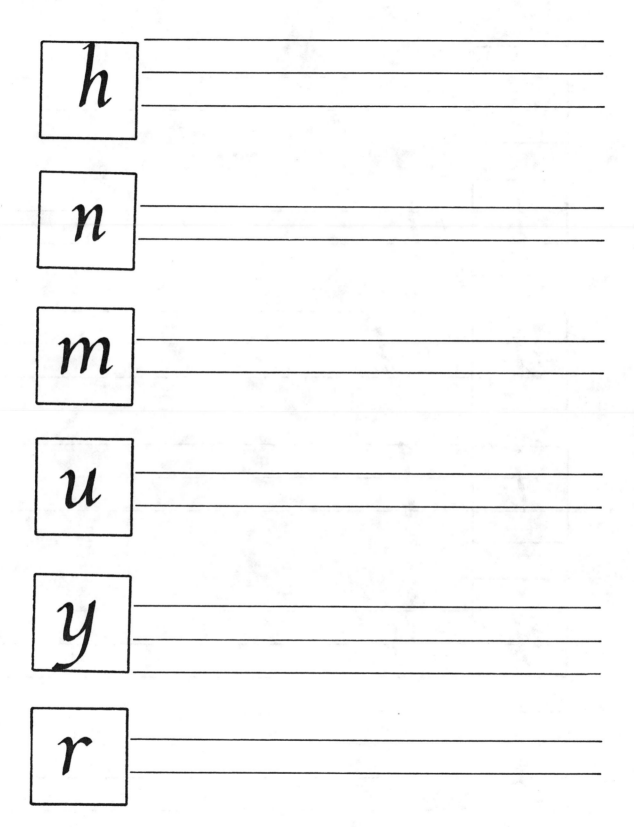

Write one line at a time and try to duplicate the examples

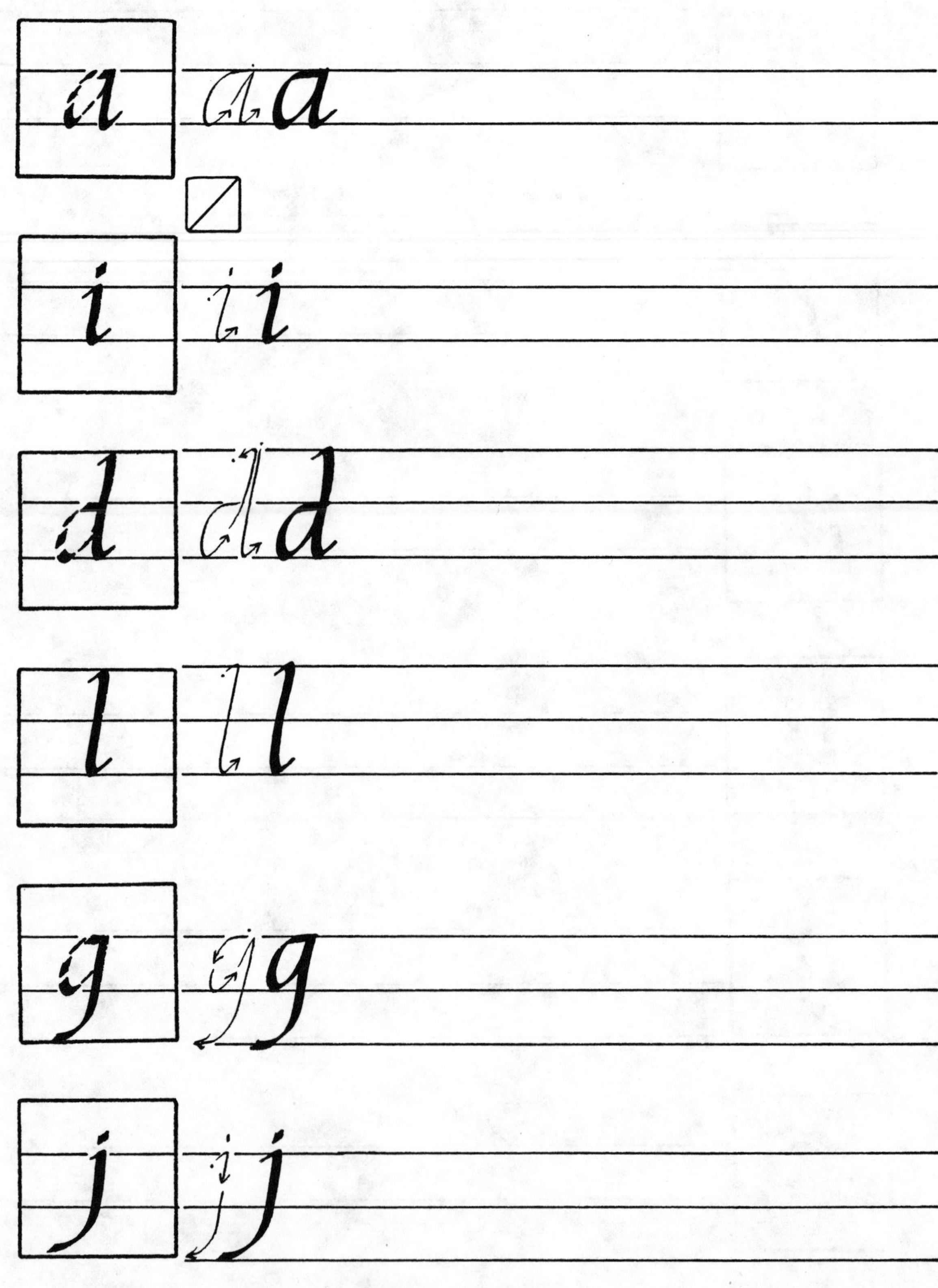

When you wrote "a" you also wrote an "i". And "d" and "l" and "g" and "j" and so on... Write these again.

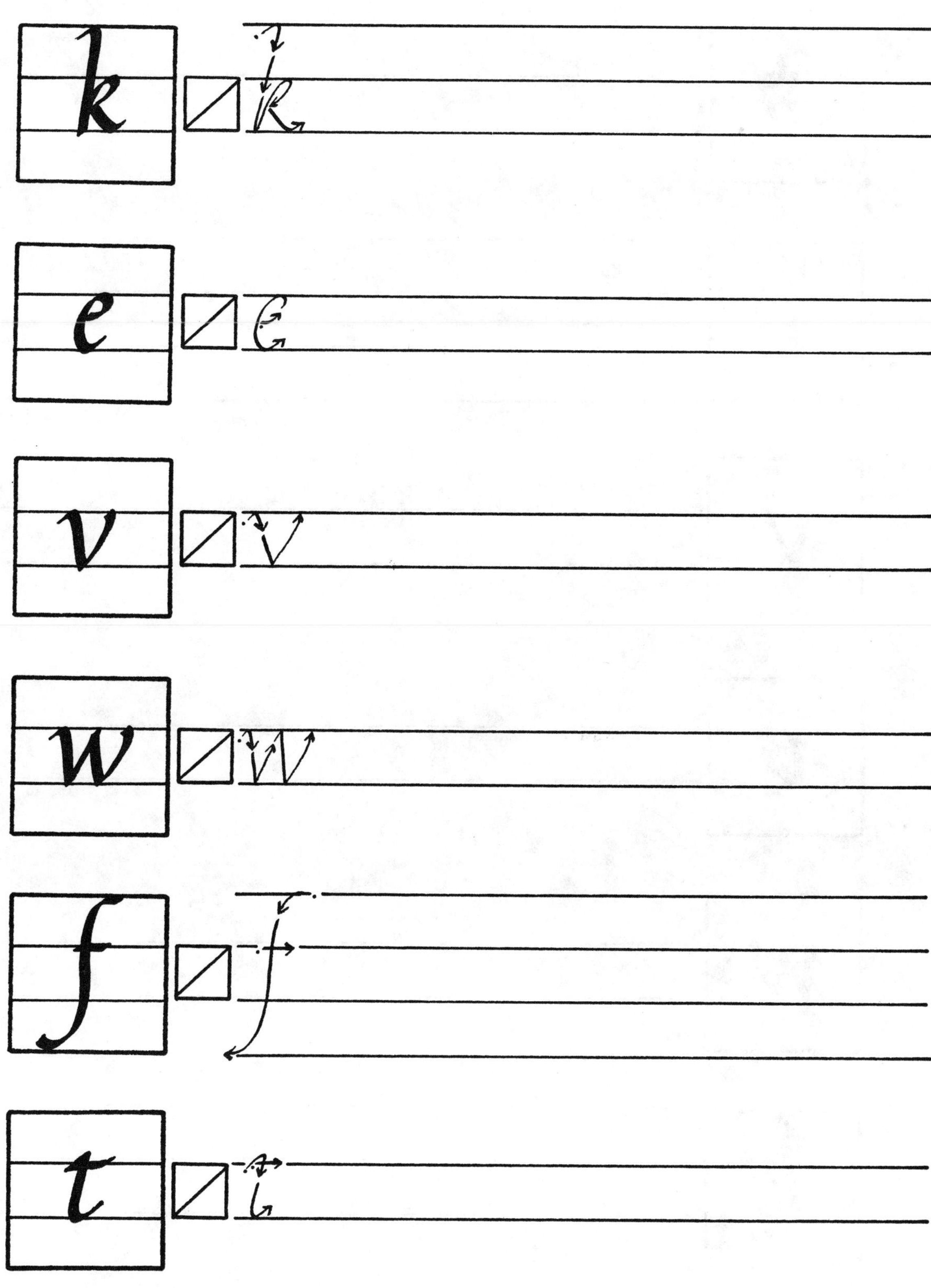

Check your pen nib angle and then write one line of each letter shown. Strive to duplicate each letter and any details.

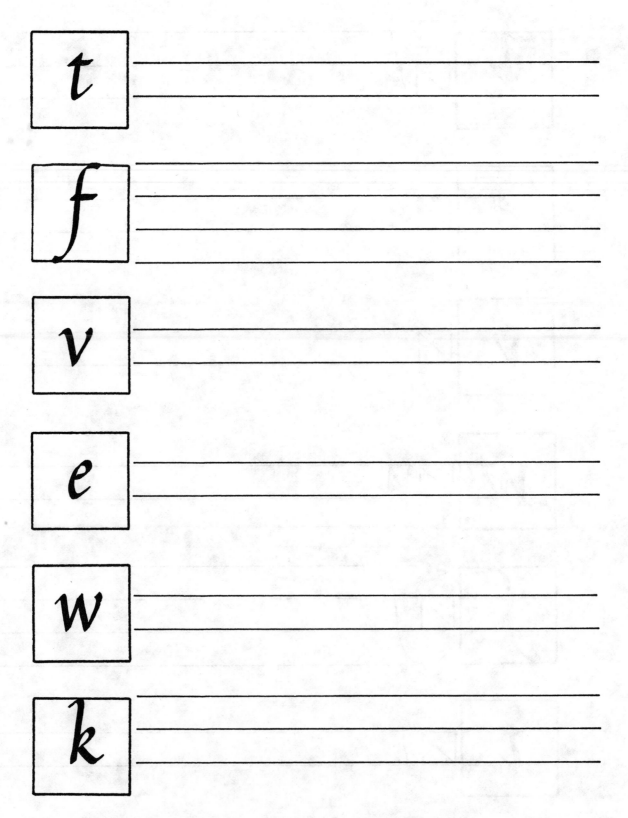

t

f

v

e

w

k

Write one line at a time. Strive to master the examples.

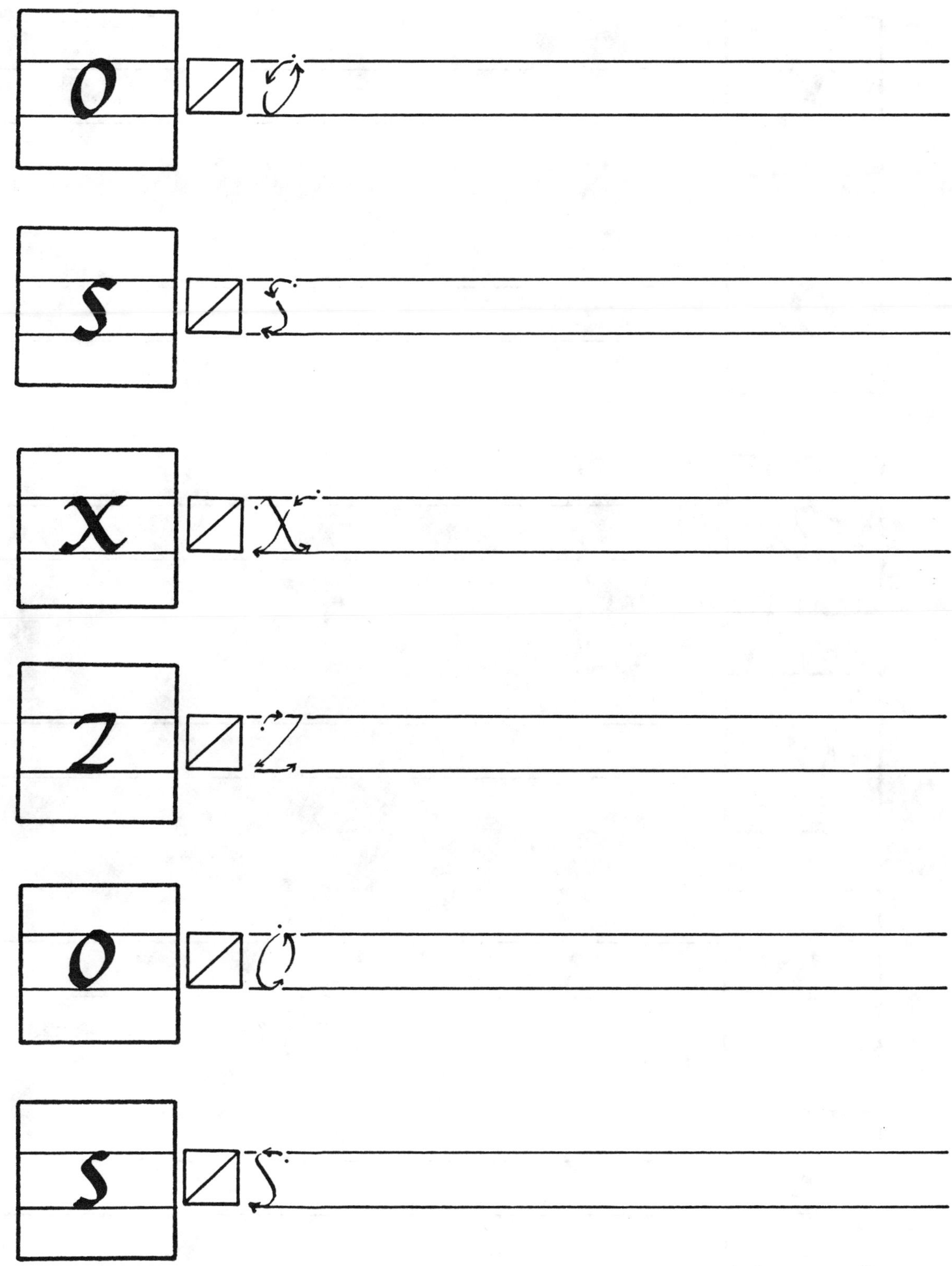

You should, by now, know the routine very well. Two of the harder forms are repeated. Write these with care.

x

o

z

o

s

s

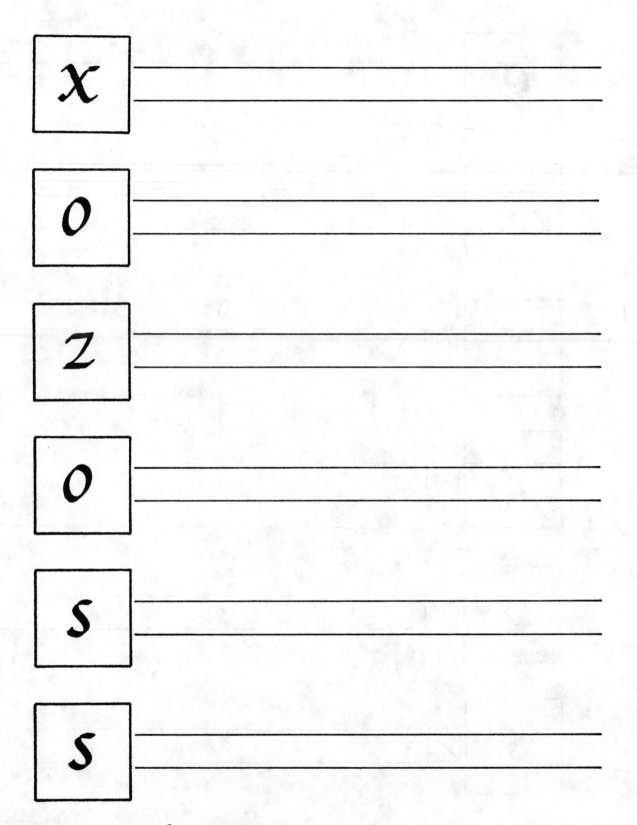

Write one line of each form shown.

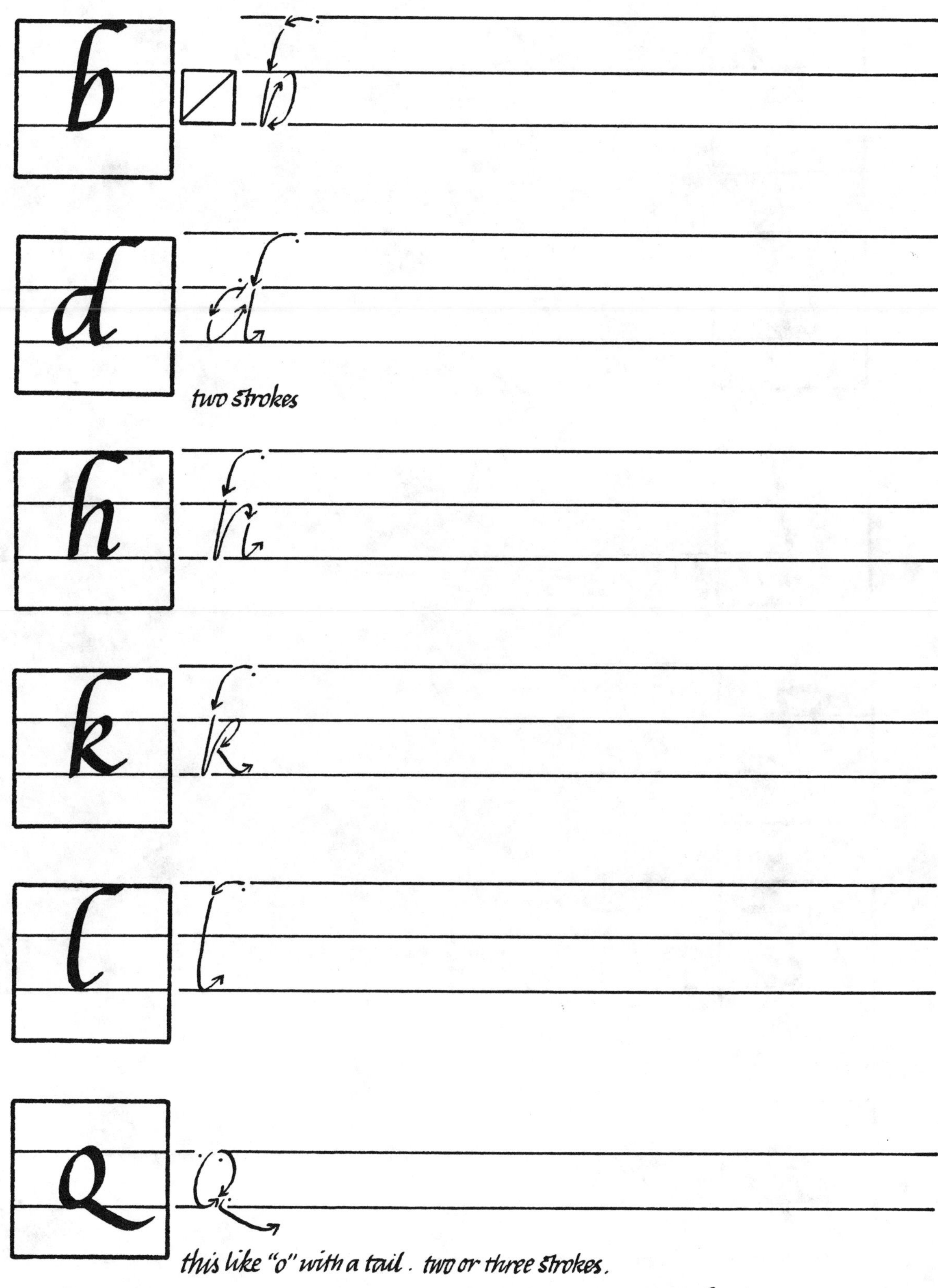
two strokes
this like "o" with a tail. two or three strokes.

Write one line of each alternate form shown. Notice that the "d" is in two strokes—starting out similar to an "a" and completed with "l."

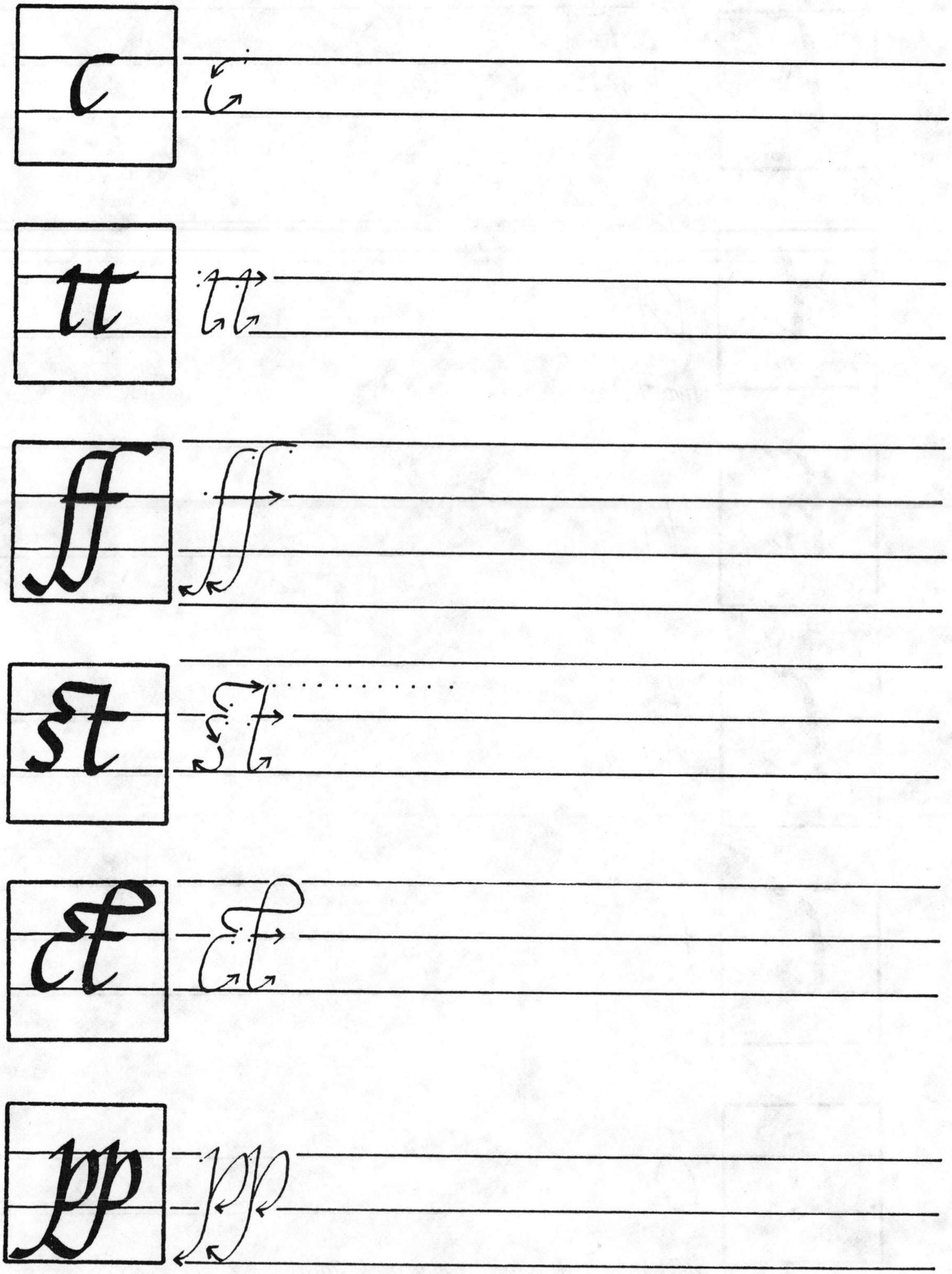

c

tt

ff

st

ct

pp

Some "ligatures" commonly used by scribes in standard italic handwriting. Check your pen nib angle— 45° please.

ft ft

ab ab

gd gd

oc oc

ke ke

Rb Rb

Capitals are not as high as ascenders are. " b, d, f, h, k, l "

The "ft" ligature. Notice 2 straight back forms are far apart "ab", a round and straight-"gd" are closer; but two rounds are closest: "oc."

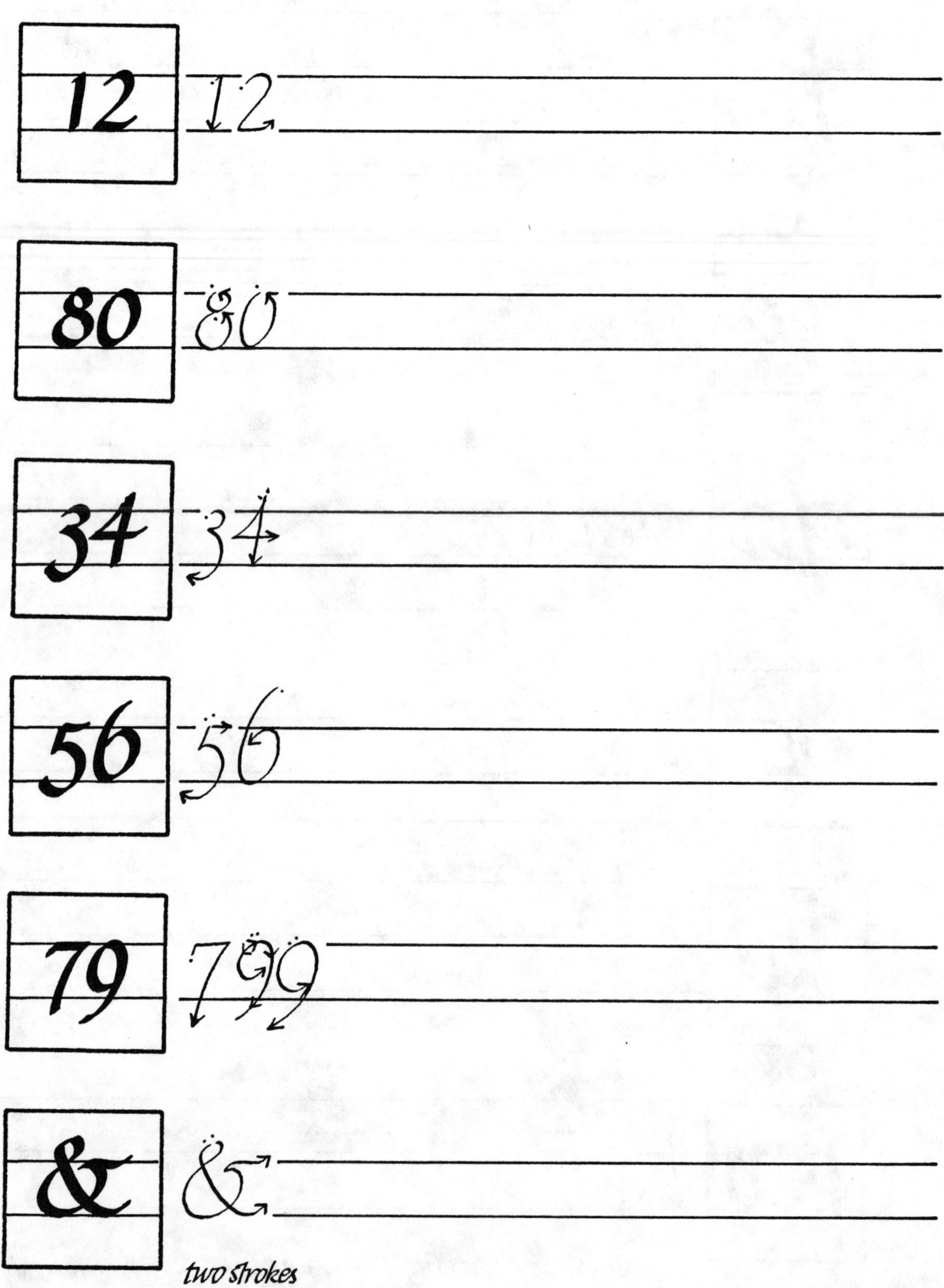

Some interesting and useful figures or numerals. Notice which ones go above or below the guide lines. And some stay between.

PART 2

A CURSIVE ALPHABET IS one which would have entry and exit strokes so that every letter could be joined together. I would not propose one. However, there are situations where "almost" every letter can be joined together. And I have shown the letters with strokes that might satisfy the cursive urge. Use only for rapid writing.

26A.

25 August 1977.

Dear Abe:

Since starting to learn writing in the Italic way, just about a year ago, my major problem has been the slope of the writing.

My pre-Italic handwriting was pretty terrible, and had a slope that would have to be labelled as running away with itself. It was (and is) an aspect requiring a great deal of discipline. While I have improved on it considerably, I still have a long way to go.

All my best

Jerry Barber

Jerry's italic is legible, though rapidly written.

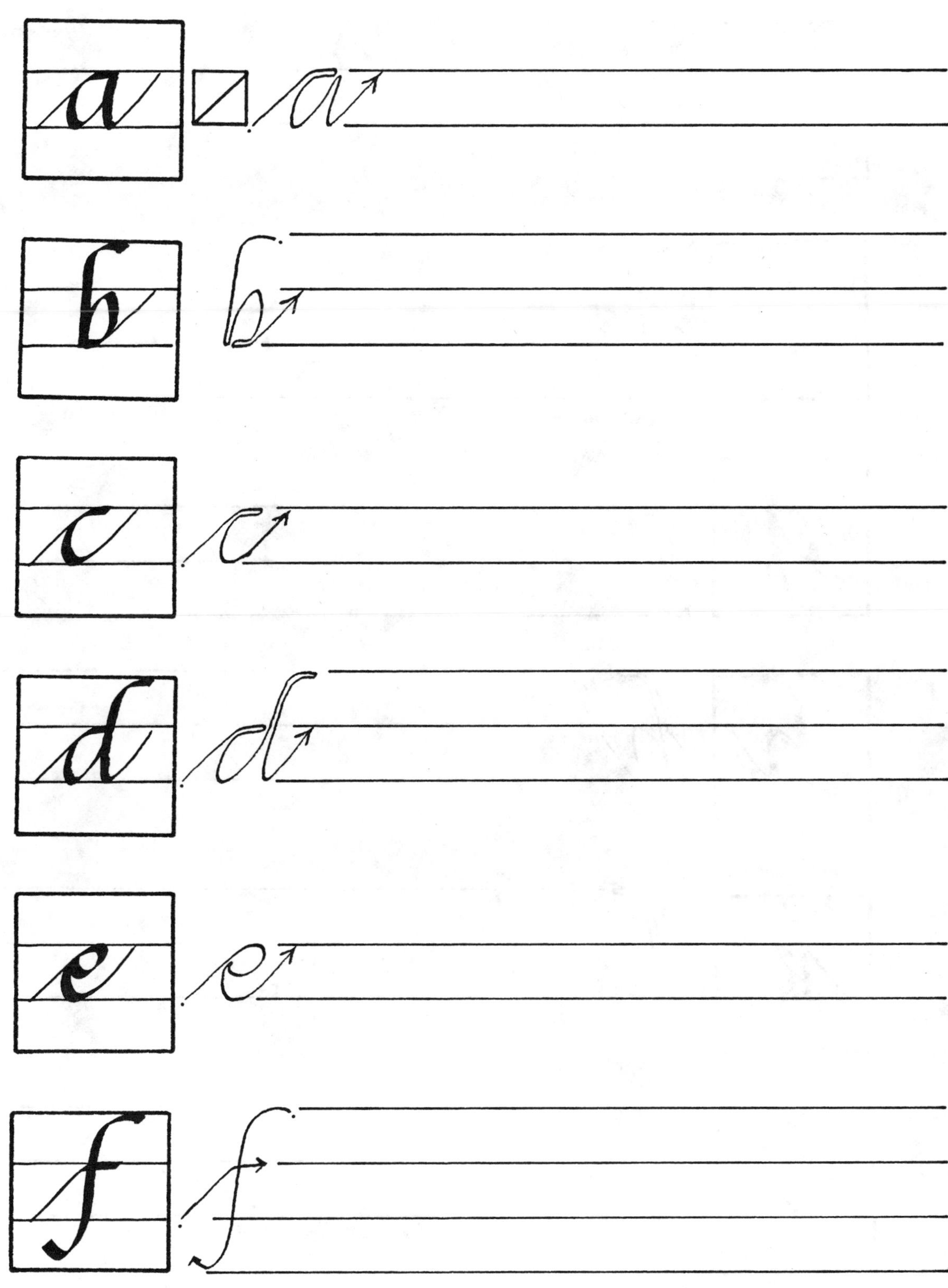

The joins are the thinnest diagonal (45°) lines; or, in "f" the join is the horizontal cross stroke. Write a line of each.

Any "double line" means to trace back over the previous stroke up. All are made in one continuous line.

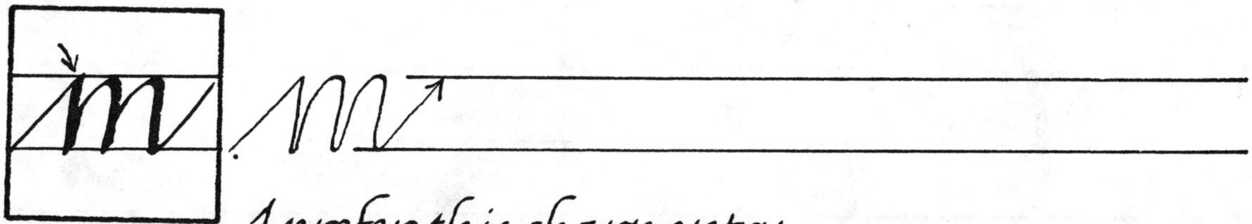

m

I prefer this sharp entry

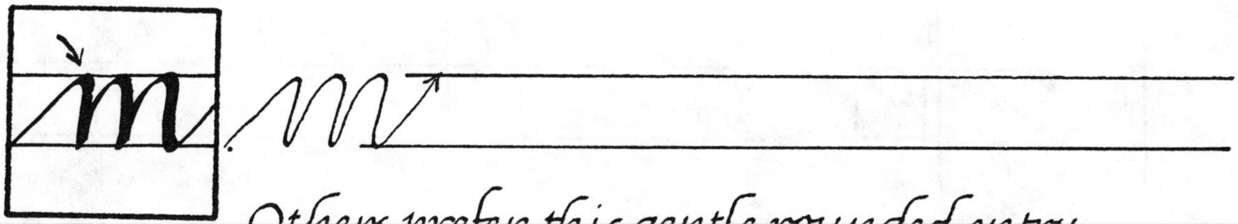

n

m

Others prefer this gentle rounded entry

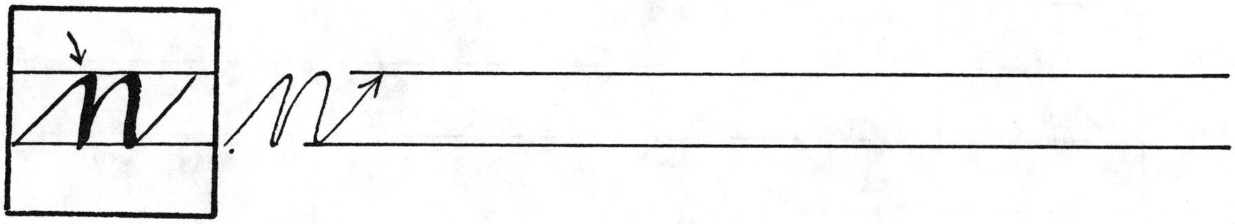

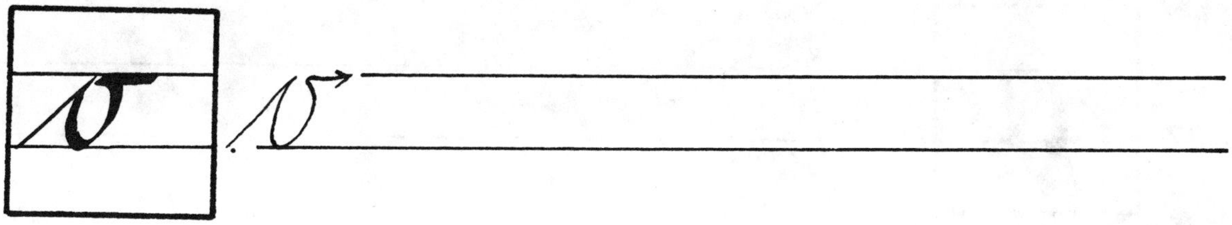

n

o

p

Write a row of each.

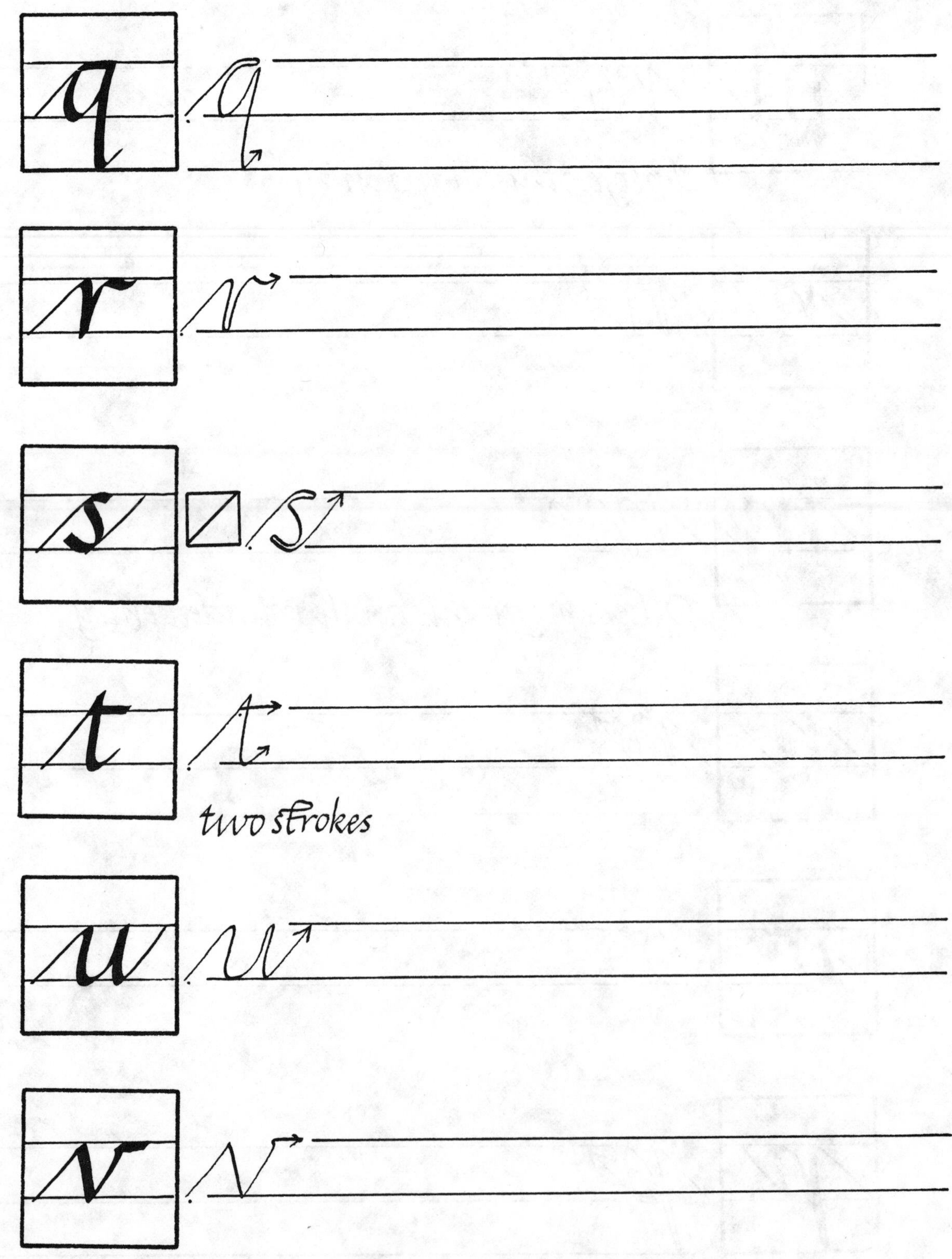

You should have noticed which letters cannot be joined "from" – as "q" cannot. Write a line of each letter shown.

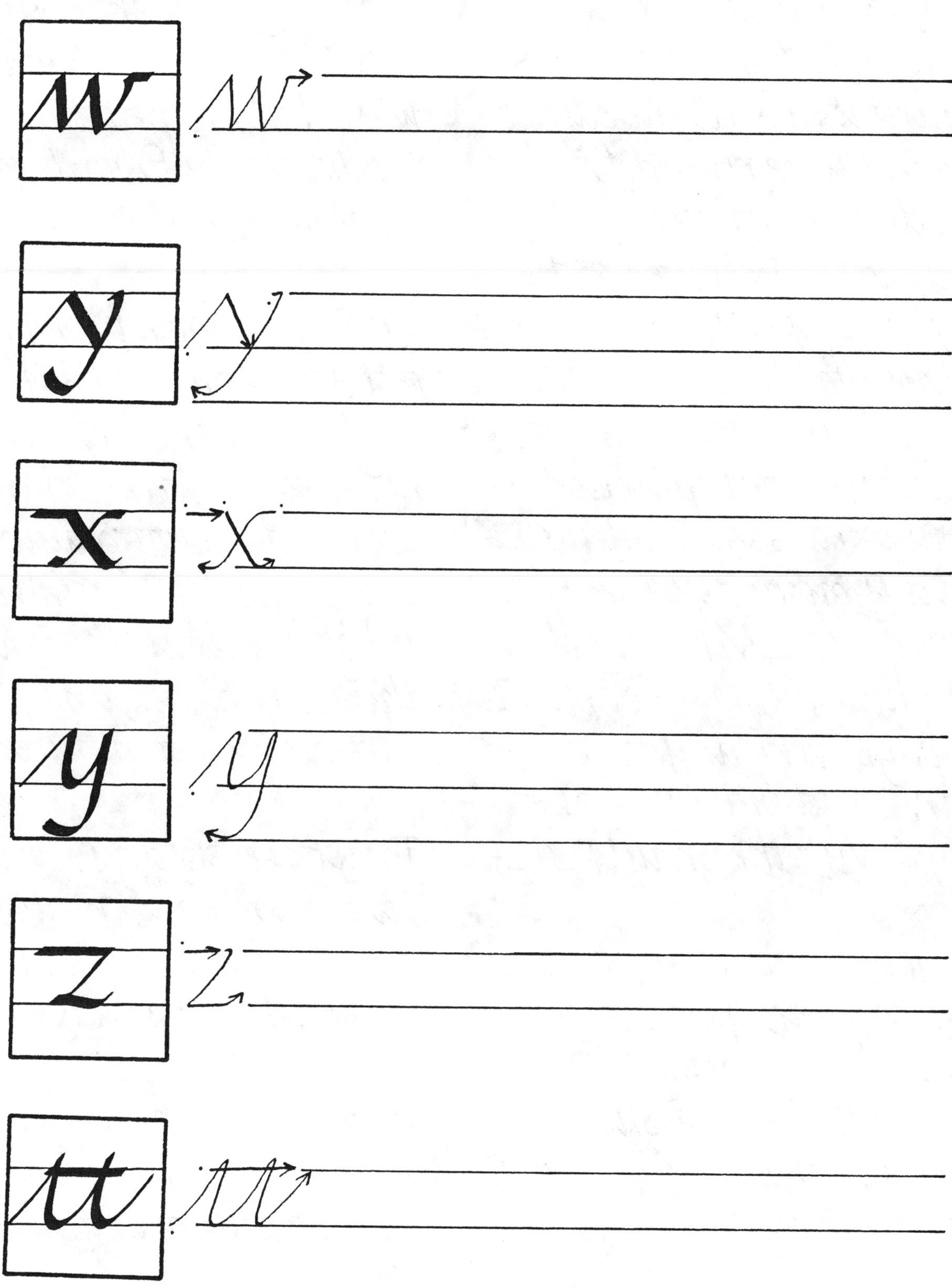

The "w" and many other letters can also be joined "to" with a horizontal line.

A further word about this cursive italic style of writing with all of the grace & beauty it has, let me say: it can easily be ruined too, if you do not practice the a.b, c's as well as strive for the perfection you'll not attain in this life time.

When the word "practice" is mentioned, some students find a thousand excuses not to practice. Marvin Coleman faithfully wrote at least one page every day for one year... and published 365 Days With the Broad Pen.

As I journey around this country and speak to students about writing, I use a variety of stories to show the relationship between how well one does something and how much time is spent in practice. "Remember your first kiss? What a letdown mine was... but as I practiced, the kiss became a favorite pass-time of mine."

Or, a man doesn't bowl a perfect 300 game unless he is at the bowling lanes for many hours every week. Hand & eye coordination requires that you practice. Kissing is a bit of hands and eyes too... I think so at least, and practice sure makes it seem nicer to me.

Practice every day... write a letter to someone. Writing is a lot nicer than using a telephone. And it is relaxing too.

Keep a notebook — a journal of your daily practice is better than no journal at all.

PART 3

A CAPITAL

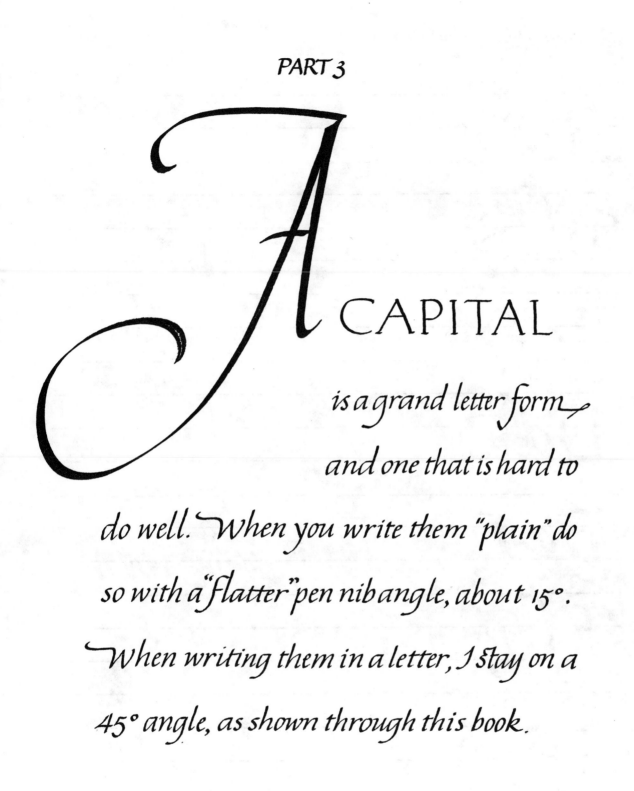

is a grand letter form and one that is hard to do well. When you write them "plain" do so with a "flatter" pen nib angle, about 15°. When writing them in a letter, I stay on a 45° angle, as shown through this book.

these capitals are on 45°

Aa A
3

Bb B
2

Cc C
1

Dd D
2

Ee E
3

Ff F
3

Gg G
2
With or without tail

Hh H
3

Try a line of Majuscules, or Capitals. Watch the height. Only 7 nibs.

Ii I
1

Jj J
1

Kk K
2

Ll L
1

Mm M
2

Nn N
2

OoQq Q
2 or 3

Pp P
2

And a row of these...

Rr R 3

Ss S 3

Tt T 2

Uu U 1

Vv 1 Ww W 1, 2, 3, or 4

Xx Yy X 2 Y 2

Zz Z 1

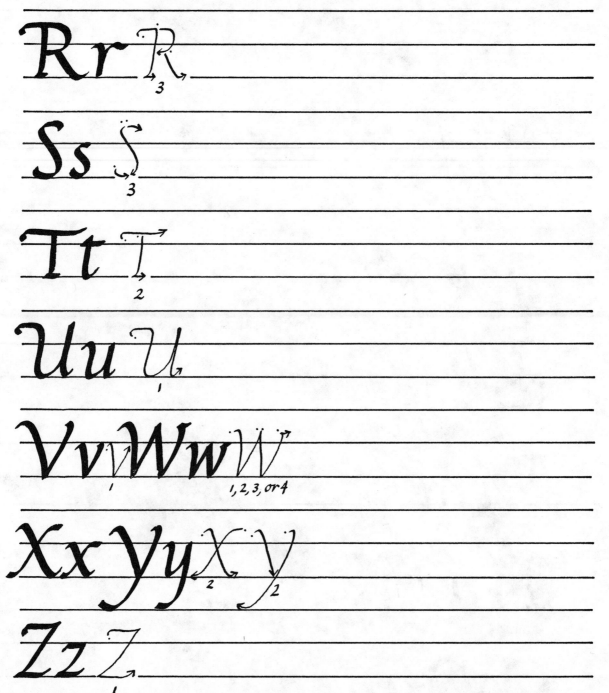

There are many variations of these. Use flourishes with care. I believe one, or two per paragraph is adequate and not distracting to the eye. Sometimes the Majuscule at the start of the first paragraph is made taller than any other letter. By the way... small letters are properly called Minuscules.

check

A

B

C

D

E

F

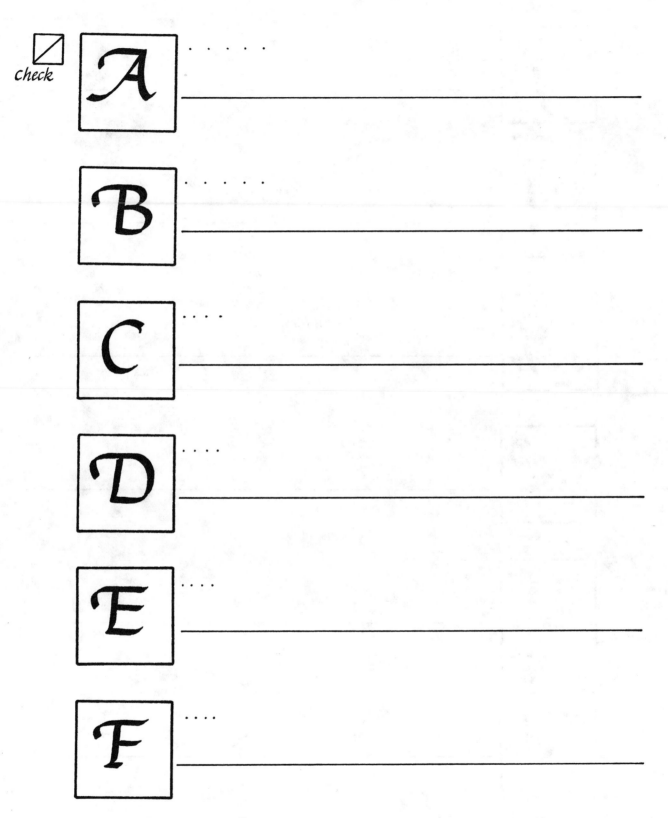

Write one row of each majuscule. Remember the height is only seven nibs.

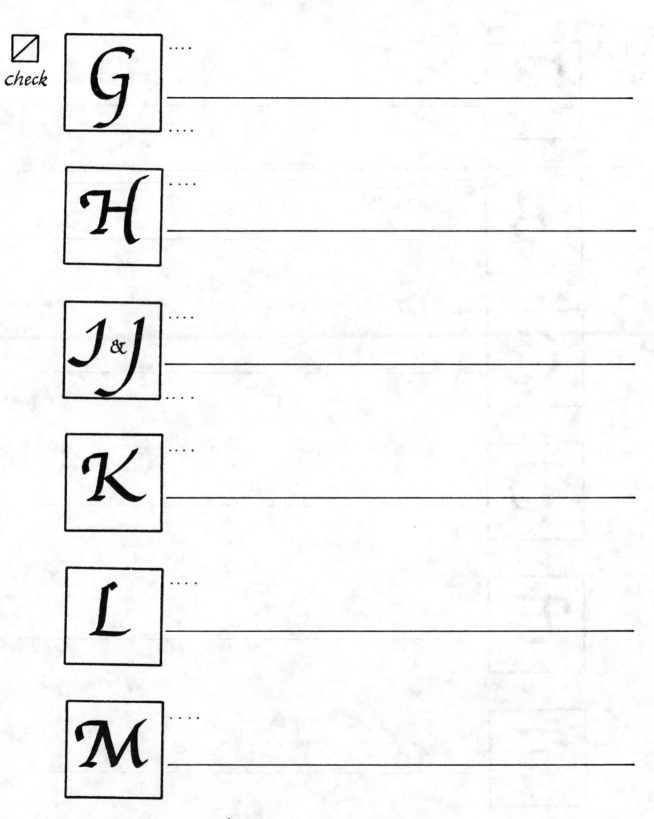

check

G

H

I & J

K

L

M

Write one row of each majuscule

Check

N

Q

P

R

S

T

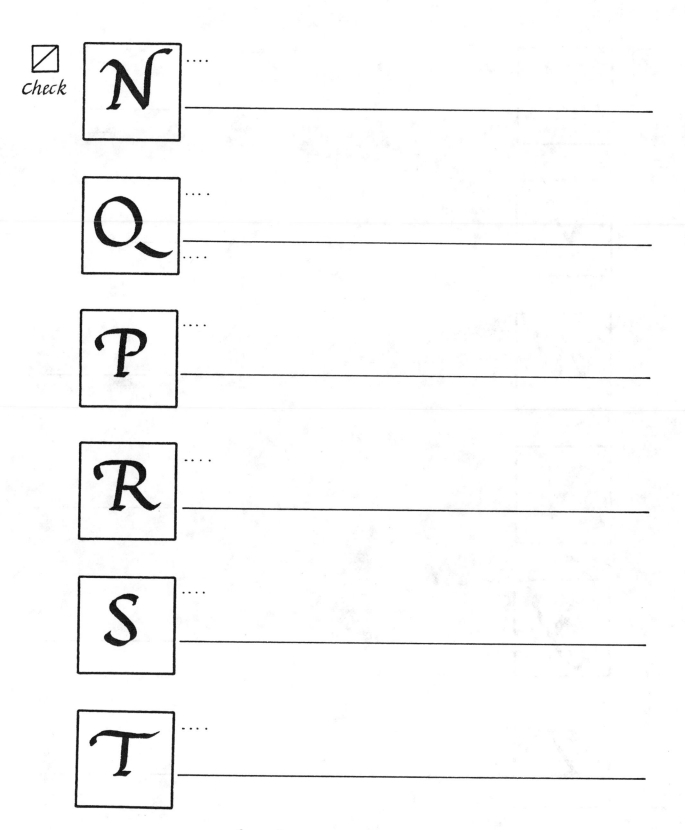

Write one row of each majuscule

check

U

V

W

X

Y

Z

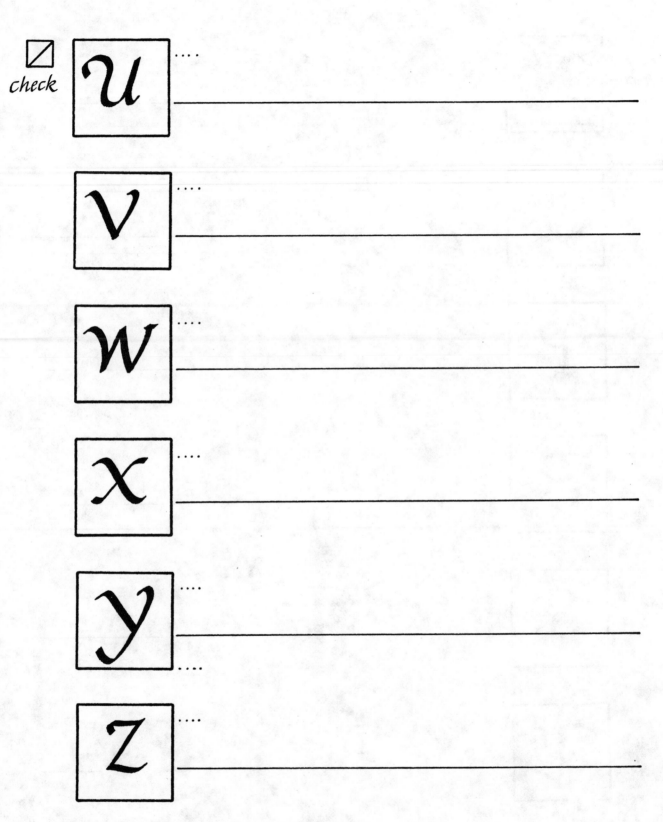

Write one row of each majuscule

ABCDEF
GHIJKL
MNOPQ
RSTUV
WXYZ
&

Z A R T D M H A

BCDEJ
FGHIJ
KLM
NPRSO
TUXA
VWYZ

Flourishes

many some last not

love sewing voyager

Quaint Queen Quack Rope

hate Oh! Happy Birthday

The quick brown fox jumped over

A A A A A A A A A A A E E E E E E E E

Experiment but always retain legibility, or make it your criterion.

An average hourly rate now being charged by calligraphers is $15.00 per hour. But these people know a little bit more than how to write the italic alphabet.

aim
aim
aim

In my opinion, the third example is the 'neatest' when written, and it is the 'fastest' to write.

You can join or not join. It is up to you to decide what you will do. All joins occur as shown in earlier assignments. Refer back if you've forgotten them.

Able, Baker and Charles. Dot, Ernest and Fay.

Gunther, Helen, Iris, Joy and Kitty. Lurton, Mae,

Nancy, Opal, Pat and Queenie. Rebecca, Sue, Tom,

Uncle Vern and Wally. Yolinda and Zelma. I forgot

the X!

X X

Use a fine nib and write a row of names between rows.

WMDQGCO — *Wide*

AHNKPRTUV — *Medium*

JBLEFSXYZ — *Narrow*

I — *Letter weight*

1234567890 — *Old style*

1234567890 — *New style*

I	II	III	IV	VI	IX	X
1	2	3	4	6	9	10

XXIV	XL	L	XC	C
24	40	50	90	100

D	DC	CM	MIV
500	600	900	1004

MCMLXXVIII 1978

Some miscellaneous information which might be of interest to you.

PART 4

SOME of the information in this part will, I trust, be useful and interesting. Assignments are useful, so try them on your own. Be creative, but accurate, and strive for perfection. Study the work of Alfred Fairbank, Raymond DaBoll, James Hayes, and all of the other examples. You can learn a lot from their work.

Soon it will be autumn
As we call it in England

Fall we call it here in
My new Homeland –
My beloved Canada!

Maples tall and golden stand
Awaiting — Nature's
Next command!

Lose thy leaves and rest
Thy soul, for Winter
Soon – to us will come!

Esme Davis was a student of the late Edward Johnston, in calligraphy; but she had not tried to write Italic until she penned these thoughts in late September.

You have made it to this page but you can go beyond this point and learn even more. So lets "write on," as they say.

Switch over to a fine pen nib. You can do this easily by flushing-out all of your old ink; and then, unscrew the larger pen nib, and screw-in the fine pen nib. Refill with ink.

You've probably noticed that I don't write "on" the lines, but rather, I write "up against" the lines.

We only read the top two-thirds of a line of writing and therefore, that much of it should be straight. The bottom doesn't matter since we do not read it, or even recognize it, while reading a sentence. If the top is straight across, and free of hooks on ascenders, we can read it rapidly without eye strain.

Can you understand? It reads: Can you understand? See my point? So write up against the line, please.

Use notebook paper with lines as wide as these—do not use the narrow ruled notebook paper.

43 Ankara Ave., Brookville, Oh., 45309
1 September 1978

Dear Mr. Fairhaven,

This is the format used by many scribes and calligraphers for writing letters. Be sure that your complete return address is at the top, followed by the date.

If you want to use that beautiful flourish when writing a letter, it is best to use it one time; either at the beginning of the paragraph, or at the end of it. You don't want to distract from the message with too many flourishes or don't you have anything important to say?

Best Wishes,

Abraham Lincoln

PS: Carpe Diem!

Letter format

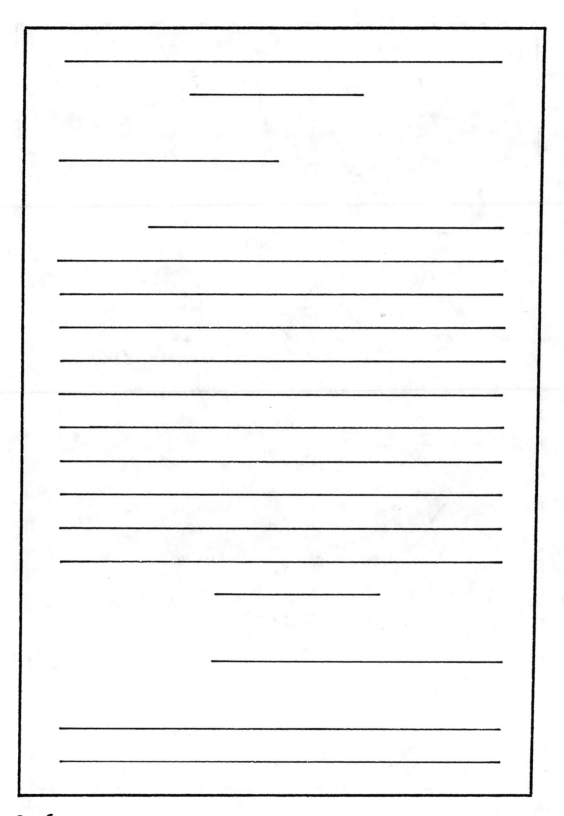

Now, it is your turn. Write a letter using the format shown.

AL
AL
AL
AL
AL
AL
AL

A.L.

1 July 1977

Hello Ben:

After a period of time, and when you're certain the people you are writing to know your full address, you can experiment with your initials and design personal stationery. Or use your full name; or, a straight design such as a pen or quill.

Now, you are well on your way, and should be having a lot of pure fun using Italic.

Fondly

Anne Langer

Letter, or note format.

Experiment with your initials on this one

Try your hand at designing a note. Refer to previous example. Try this one without guide lines

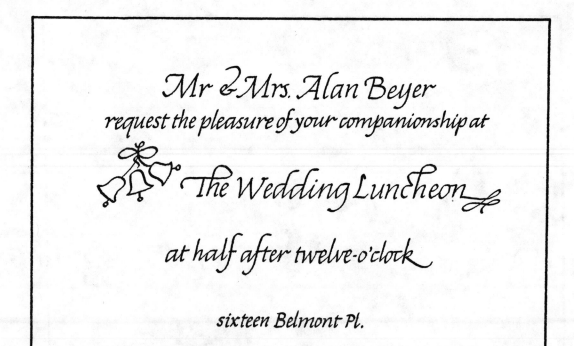

Mr & Mrs. Alan Beyer
request the pleasure of your companionship at

The Wedding Luncheon

at half after twelve-o'clock

sixteen Belmont Pl.

Use a fine nib and design an invitation
use very light pencil guide lines, and erase them when done

TRY SOMETHING WACKY...

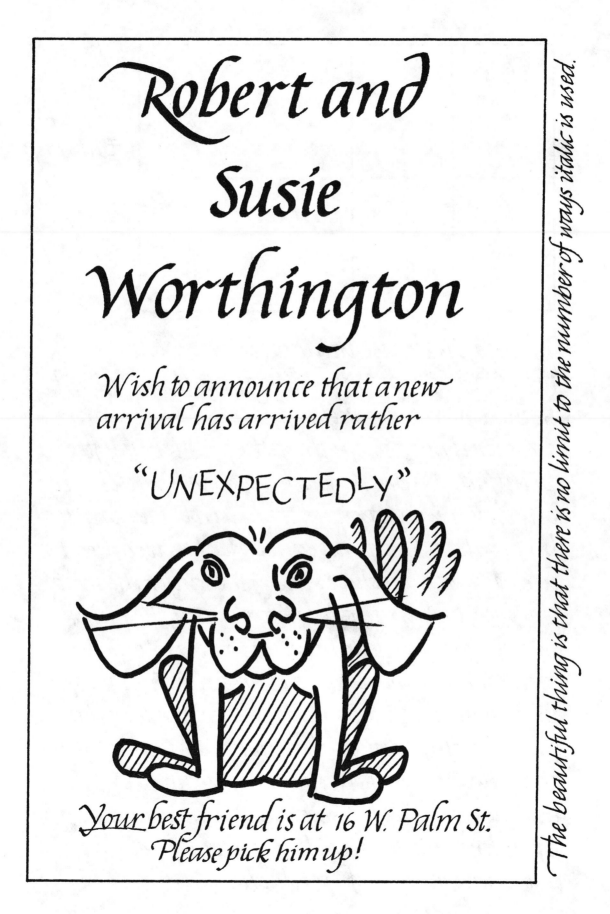

Robert and Susie Worthington

Wish to announce that a new arrival has arrived rather

"UNEXPECTEDLY"

Your best friend is at 16 W. Palm St. Please pick him up!

The beautiful thing is that there is no limit to the number of ways italic is used.

Some Paper and Printing Information

$8\frac{1}{2}$×11"		
		11×17"

This sheet would be $22\frac{1}{2}$×34". or 23×35" But it is cut down into 6 sheets, in this sample.

When you do use italic on a job which is going to be printed, you should begin to think about using correct size sheets of paper. Use the same sizes for your design that the printer uses for printing. Paper is made into rolls which are cut down into various standard sizes for use by printers. Printing equipment is designed to use these various sheet sizes. The larger the sheet of paper, the larger, and more costly, the printing press has to be to handle it. Most "quickie" printers use duplicators that operate from paper plates, which are electrostatically exposed, and the 'press' usually cannot accomodate paper larger than "legal" size sheets; but some do have 'presses' that handles 11×17" sheets. Get acquainted with a printer in your area. They can really help you, and save you a lot of headaches later on.

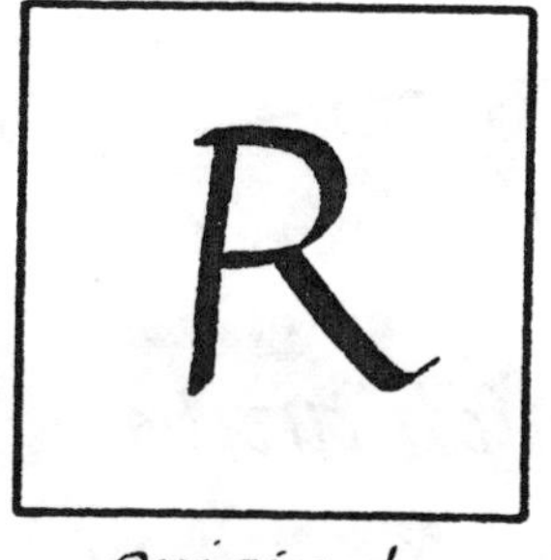

Original

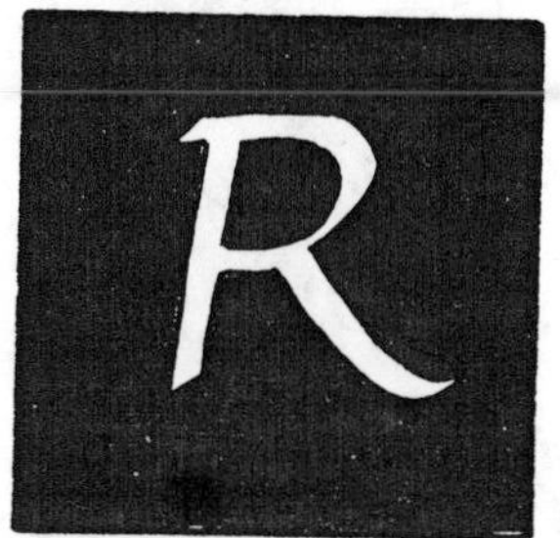

Reversed

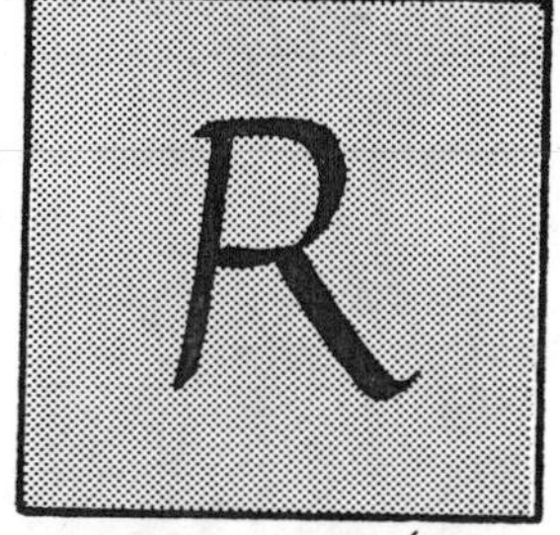

Screened

Only square was reversed

Half & Half

Your calligraphy should be done in black ink on white paper. But you can simply ask your printer to "reverse it" and then you have it printed.

What you'll end up with is a black page, or a black spot on a white page. If a sheet of paper is used the letters on it appear white. You could tell him to run it in red, but you might pay a fee to wash the press so that red ink can be used. Or, ask him to screen it. And, always ask how much any operation costs before you have him do the job. The example at left is a "55 line screen at 30%." It could be 10% up to nearly 100%. Never be afraid to ask questions. You will be amazed at how much you can learn — if you ask. So ask questions.

Printing presses have 'fingers' which grabs the paper and pulls it through the machine. So you cannot have the entire sheet of paper inked completely over, because the fingers grab about ¼" of its edge. So you must allow a "gripper" area along one edge. (finger/gripper) This non-inked area can be cut or trimmed off by the printer. Of course, the sheet size will be reduced by the amount trimmed off.

gripper area is not printed; but can be trimmed off.

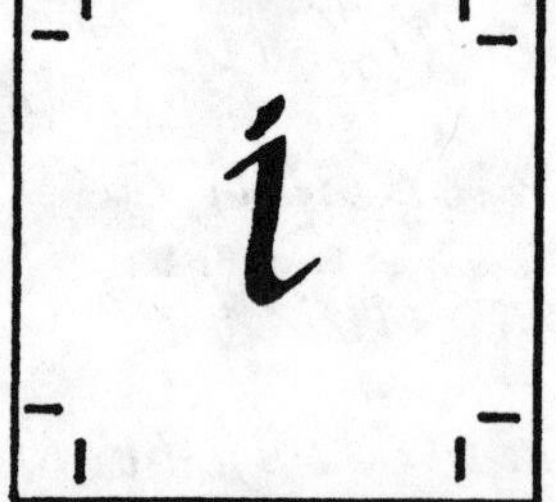

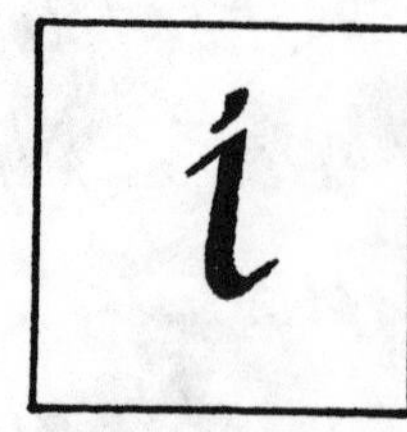

By "cropping," color can go to edge. This could be reversed out to the very edge. (Or screened)

Art prepared on oversize sheet. With (4) corner trim marks. The Job is printed on larger sheet, excess is cut away. In this way the size left after trimming is the desired size

Caution

"Ink is being used here!"

Permanent: Long lasting · doesn't fade

only means that you can't remove all of it from your clothes. But, it will smear, if touched by a finger, when its on paper.

India:

when it is dry, it won't smear or even wash off of paper. It will be the safest to use. Use it on commissioned works. Use only with dip pens, quills, or reed pens and brushes.

Tip:

clean out pens with 4 parts water, 1 part ammonia & 1 part liquid detergent.

Questions and some answers...

most often asked by our students

How long does it take to learn?

SEVERAL STUDIES HAVE SHOWN that twenty-one days are required to change habitual action patterns involving hand & eye coordination. It is similar to reprogramming a computer in several respects. But...

THE ALPHABET CAN BE TAUGHT IN just a few minutes by a skilled teacher, but, any student must also master what he is taught, if it is to be of any lasting value. And therefore, the question is answered by each student. To master it will require several more days than twenty-one! Several years, in some cases, would be normal.

STUDENTS DEVELOP SKILLS IN handwriting and naturally progress from one level to the next. The elusive ultimate peak has been described by Raymond DaBoll. He says it is "Disciplined Freedom." That is an adequate description.

Can I earn money doing it?

THIS QUESTION IS THE SINGLE ONE most often asked of us. Yes, people do earn money using improved writing skills in most cases, and real calligraphy in the others. The City of Los Angeles paid their calligrapher just over $31,000.00 for one year.

A MAJORITY OF CALLIGRAPHERS DO work on a part time basis only, and whatever they earn in these arrangements is a lot less than a full-time calligrapher earns. It is a supplement to other income usually.

Where can one obtain work?

THERE ARE MANY DIFFERENT PLACES where a skilled scribe or calligrapher can find work to do. Ad agencies are always looking for people to do hand lettering. Card companies and printing houses use qualified people and so do publishers. There are many others too.

What about calligraphy as fine art?

A LOT OF PEOPLE ARE STRIVING TO COMbine calligraphy and fine art. Some have been successful. Most haven't. Usually the best work is accomplished by those knowing a lot about both areas, and by avoiding extremes.

Where can I see calligraphy?

ST. JOHNS UNIVERSITY IS A GOOD place to start out. The Hill Monastic Manuscript Library, Bush Center, in Collegeville, Minnesota, has a rare variety of manuscripts on film. In this way, you can see the variety and determine what you want to see elsewhere. Chicago's Newberry Library has a collection you might want to study & there are, of course, many others.

237 Elmers Avenue, Ashburton, Surrey.
12 July.

Dear Elsie,

To-day Uncle Fred met us at Charing Cross and showed us the sights of Whitehall. We saw the Admiralty, the War Office, the Treasury and other important Government offices. Then Uncle took us into the museum of the Royal United Service Institution, in the Banqueting House, to see the relics & models.

We came out into Whitehall again just in time to see the sentries changed at the Horse Guards. What splendid horses!

After we left the Cenotaph we watched the curious antics of the pelicans in St. James Park. That was fun!

Your loving brother,
John.

Miss E. Richard.

THE WOODSIDE WRITING CARD, No. 6

This original 1931 card was generously provided by Mr. Alfred Fairbank, and is an example of his writing.

Dear Abe:

I find a certain amount of lateral compression will aid in the execution of Italic handwriting. Compression of strokes does several things. It accentuates the words, the lines, the slant of the writing and the text design on the page. And, of course, the word count in a given space.

However, when compression is used the individual letters must be carefully formed to maintain legibility.

Good luck in your venture.

Cordially yours

James Hayes

Mr. Hayes has been a professional scribe, author, and teacher of calligraphy for many years.

DOGWOOD

One of the worlds finest flowering trees, this floral emblem of British Columbia reaches heights of up to sixty feet. Breathtaking in May and June with thousands of creamy white blossoms, these spectacular trees are again delightful in September and October when the heavily veined, wavy-edged leaves turn a harmonious blend of deep reds, purple and pink. At the same time, the creamy bracts having fallen, the true flower-heads are replaced by clusters of drupes, all brilliant scarlet, edged with orange. Then the tree is indeed incredibly beautiful.

PACIFIC DOGWOOD Cornus Nutallii

Martin Jackson · Vancouver · Canada · For Abraham Lincoln · 24·8·77

Martin Jackson is a professional calligrapher from Canada.

QUI bene bibit · bene dormit · Qui bene dormit non cogitat non malum ⁘ Qui cogitat non malum numquam peccat ⁘ Qui numquam peccat + salvandum est ⁘ Ergo ~ qui bene bibit + salvandum est ·

Scripsit · Irene Alexander · 1977
North Vancouver · BC · Canada

Who drinks well · sleeps well.
Who sleeps well · thinks no evil · who thinks no evil · has peace of mind
Who has peace of mind · shall be saved · Therefore who drinks well · shall be saved

Irene Alexander is another professional from Canada

June 29, 1977

Dear Mr. Lincoln,

I have enjoyed every minute of my Italic course and have also appreciated your compliments — thankyou! At your request, I am writing this letter in my newly acquired style of writing and am enclosing my photograph. Good luck with your new book — I shall be anxious to see it when it becomes available. My next lessons will follow shortly.

Sincerely,
Arlyne Gonczewski

A Former correspondence-course student of ours!

Dear Abraham, The ABC Book arrived yesterday and it is a beautiful book, I'm glad to have it in my collection. Your recent letter is so unique that I have framed it for everyone to enjoy. Best Wishes from all of us. ~Ann

Ann Kette's Celtic Knot.

Dear Abraham

Thank you for a truly inspirational letter. I have really worked hard since seeing the beauty of your hand.

You're going to an awful lot of bother to help me, let me say sincerely how very much I appreciate it.

We were really glad to have you visit on your recent tour. It's still the talk of the town.

Your friend in writing!

Buddy Blackwell

Buddy writes this style better than anyone I know, and does it this way most of the time.

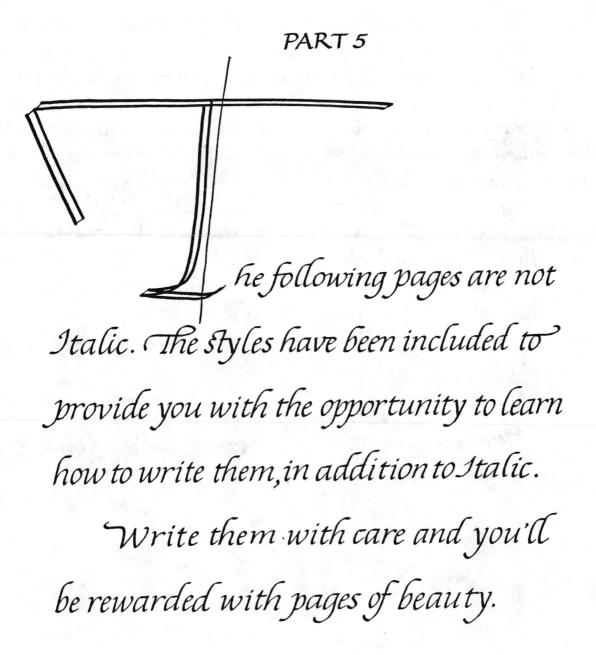

PART 5

The following pages are not Italic. The styles have been included to provide you with the opportunity to learn how to write them, in addition to Italic.

Write them with care and you'll be rewarded with pages of beauty.

We have come thus to the central problem of all art. The great Chinese general and premier, Tseng Kuofan, said in one of his family letters that the only two living principles of art in calligraphy are form and expression, and that one of the greatest calligraphers of the time, Ho Shaocki, approved of his formula and appreciated his insight. Since all art is concrete, there is always a mechanical problem, the problem of technique, which has to be mastered, but as art is also spirit, the vital element in all forms of creation is the personal expression. It is the artist's individuality, over and against his mere technique, that is the only significant thing in a work of art. — *Lin Yutang*

Written out by Marion Andrews ~ Calligrafree,
Copyright 1974. Brookville, Oh.

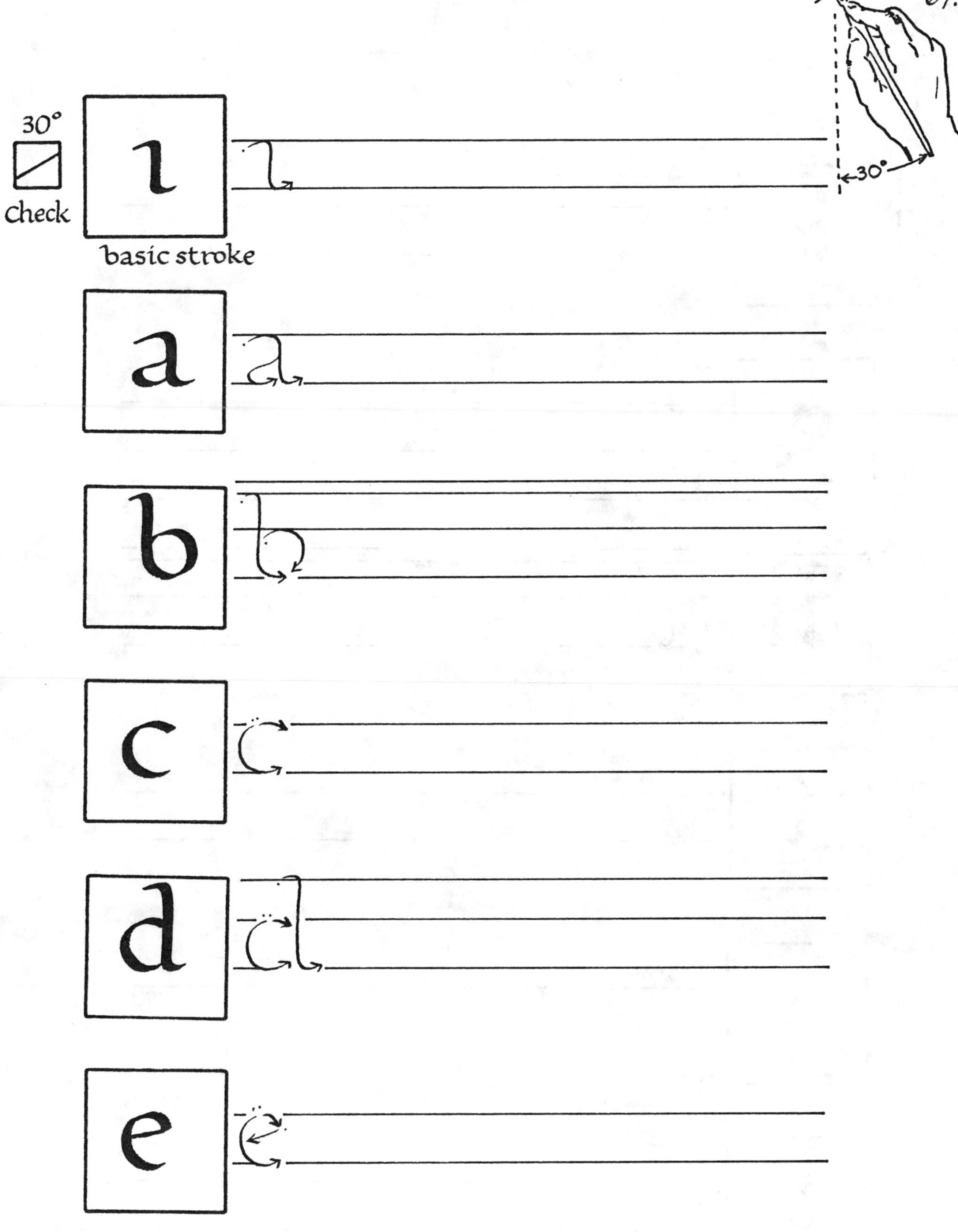

The pen angle changes to 30° for Roman Bookhand. *Notice* that the ascenders are only 4 units high, and

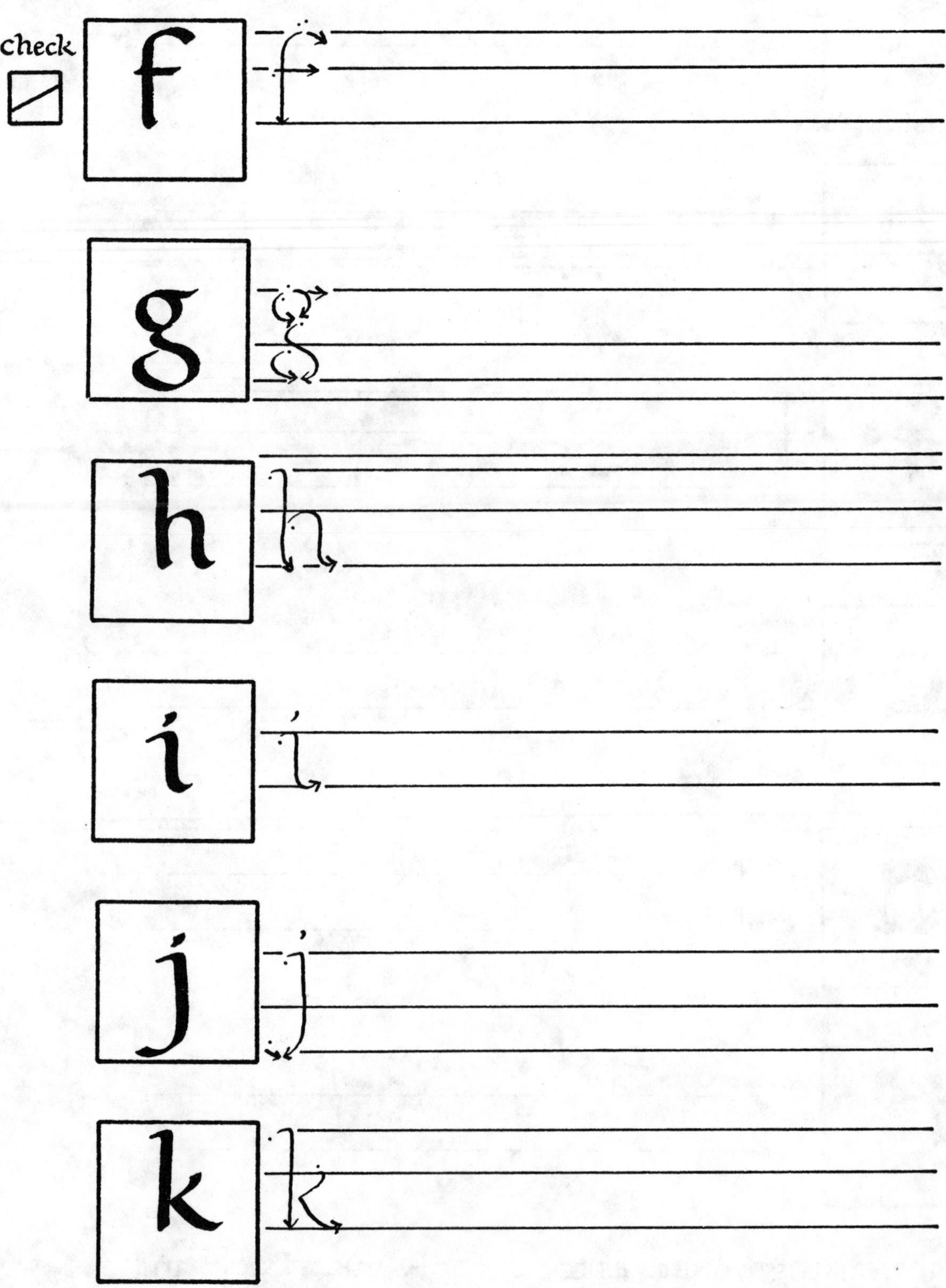

the main body is 5 units -*nibs*- high and the descenders are 3 units deep. *Write a row of each.*

check

l

m

n

o

p

q

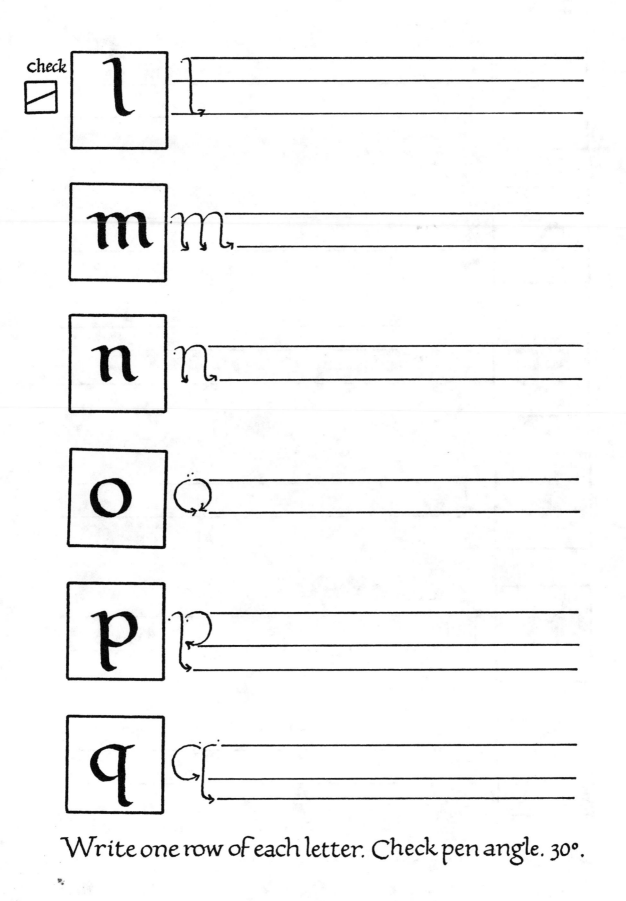

Write one row of each letter. Check pen angle. 30°.

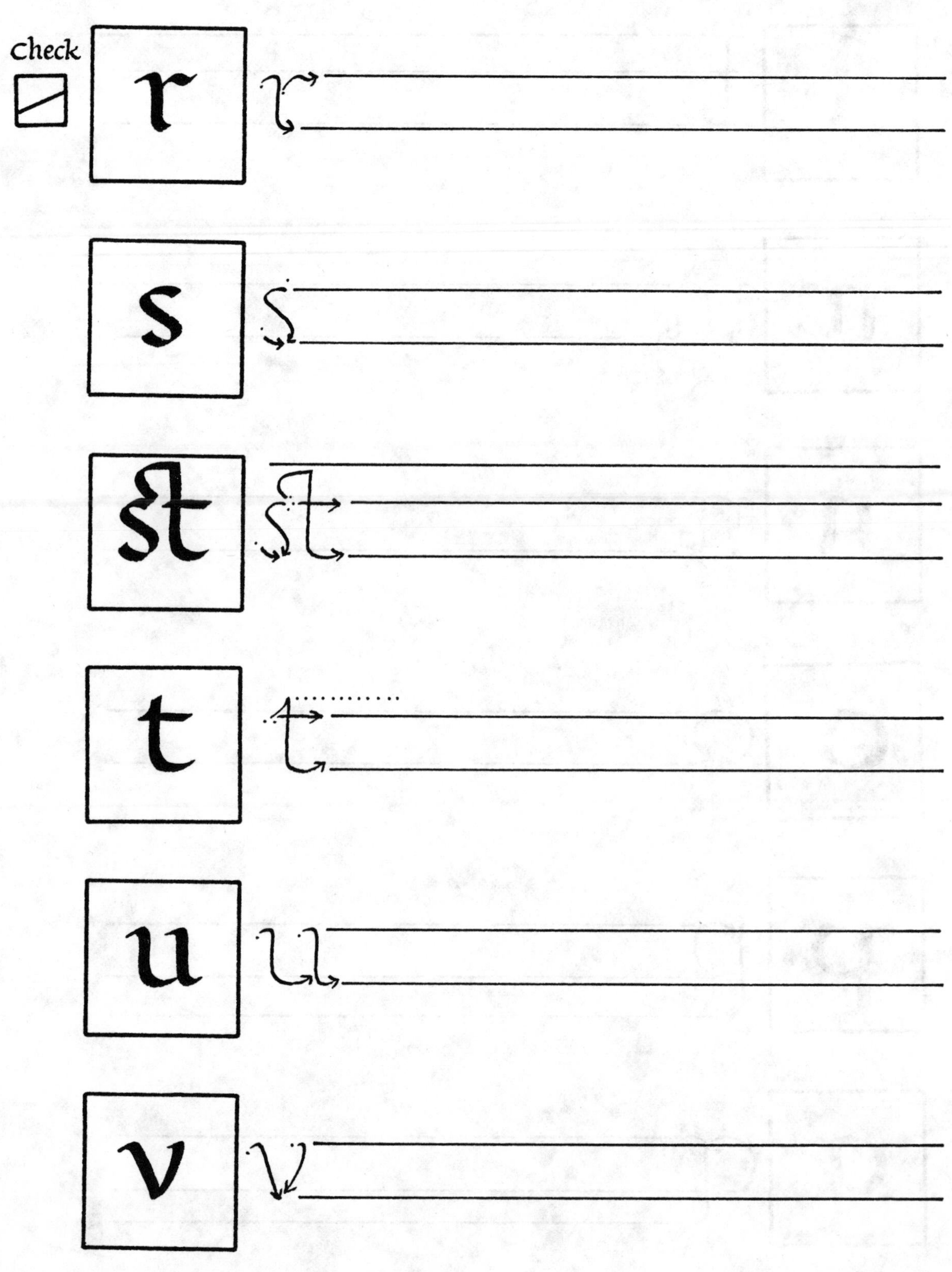

One row of each letter.

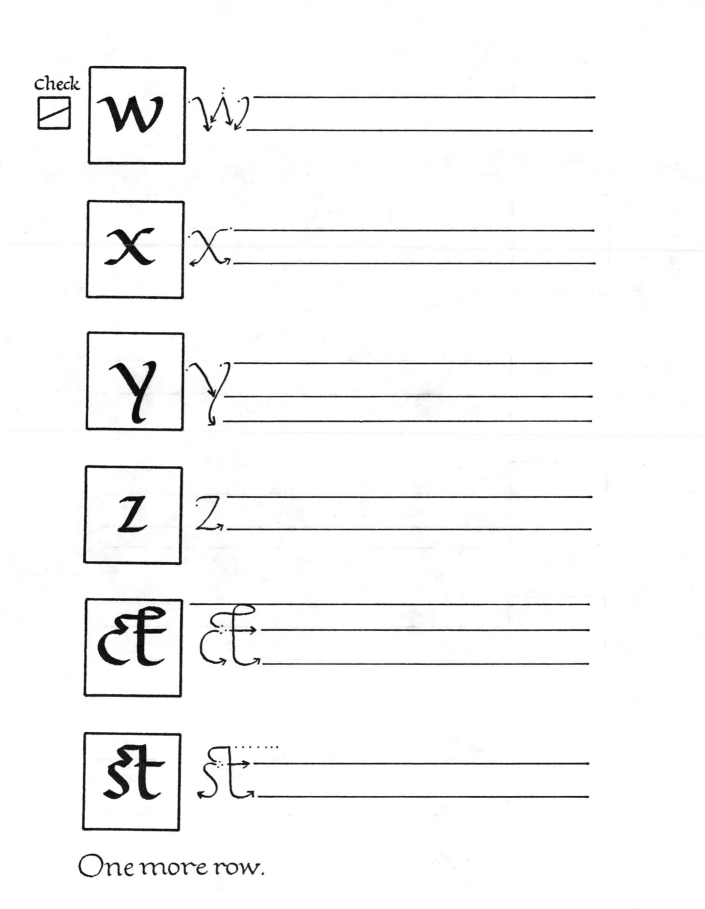

Check

w

x

y

z

ct

st

One more row.

Practice, or, make-up sheet

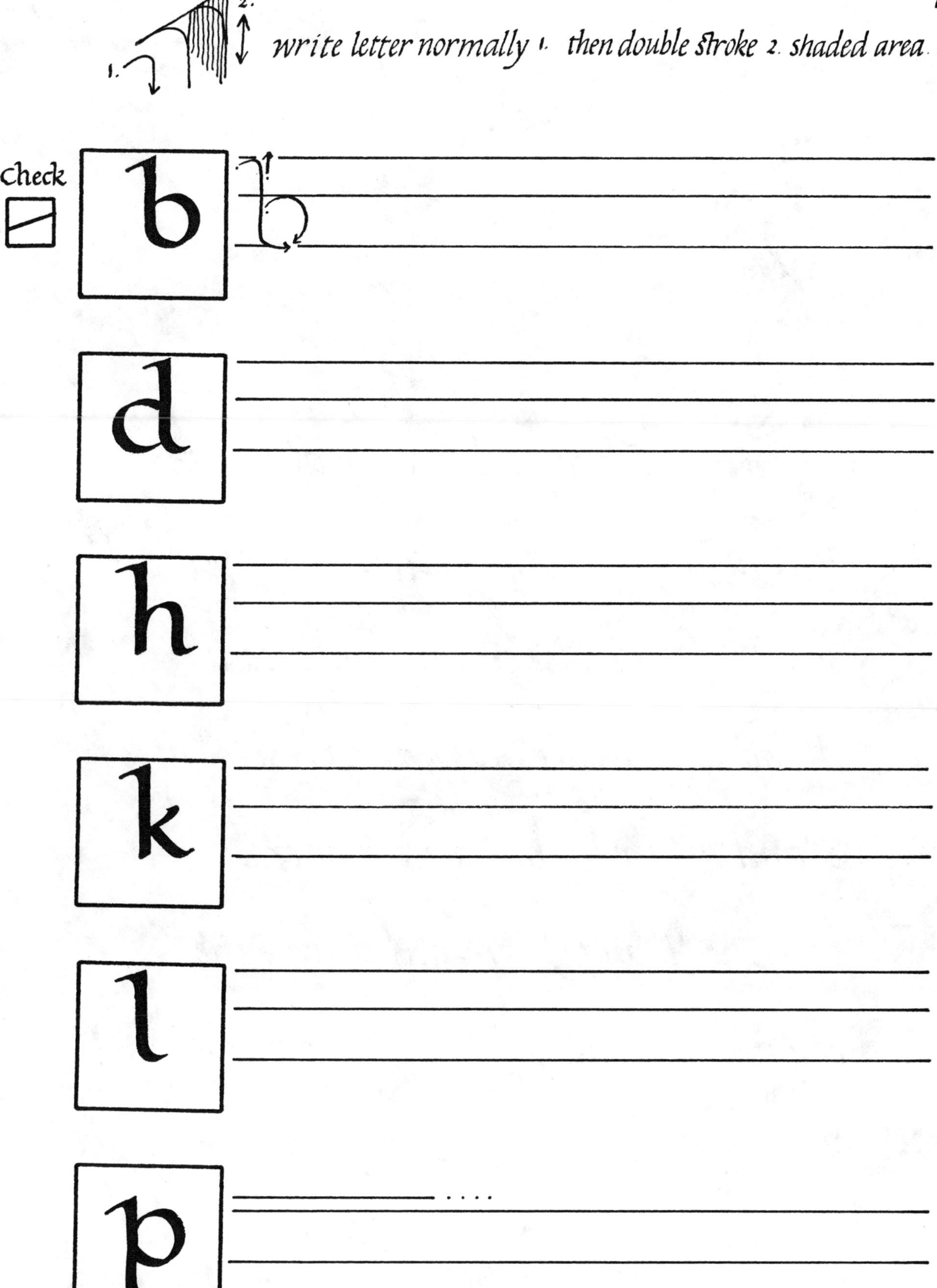

Alternate heads - serifs - on ascenders & descenders

Make one row of each letter.

PART 6

Rustic capitals are rapidly written and are fit for dignified use. The pen slant is 75° and letters are compressed. All horizontals are heavy and crosses on "e" and "h" are high. There is no cross on "a." The "l" and "f" are tallest and the counters, or loops, of "p" and "r" are small. Vertical strokes are twisted to fat bottoms.

Rustic · Pen Angle is 75°

A

B

C

D

E

begin twisting the pen from vertical about midway down on all vertical strokes. Markers give best results for the new student. Do not cross the "A" form

the "f" is like "e" but taller. The "h" cross is high. You can use 3 spaces of wide ruled notebook paper for practice

the "L" is taller than "I", to avoid confusion, but they are alike in other respects.

P
Q
R
S
T
V

Remember, no cross on "A", and, "F and L" are higher than the other letters.

ALTERNATE STYLE

Basic Stroke

A B C D E F G H I I J K L M
N O P Q R S T U V W X Y Z

STEEP PEN ANGLE · A TWISTING MOTION NOT REQUIRED · RUSTIC

PART 7

Chancery italic, carolingian and the uncial styles, on the following pages, are for practice only. There are many variations of each style and those styles are available in other books for you to study. Ask your instructor about them.

&ABCDEFGHIJKLMNOPQRSTU
VWXYZ

chancery italic

abcdefgh ← the "h" tucks back

ijklmnop the "k" has a foot

qrssſtuv an alternate on q is "Q"

wxyyz two forms on y; the latter is best.

st · ct ct · st · tt · ff · ff · gg · & 1234567890

& A compressed style. See: "Three Classics of Italian Calligraphy."

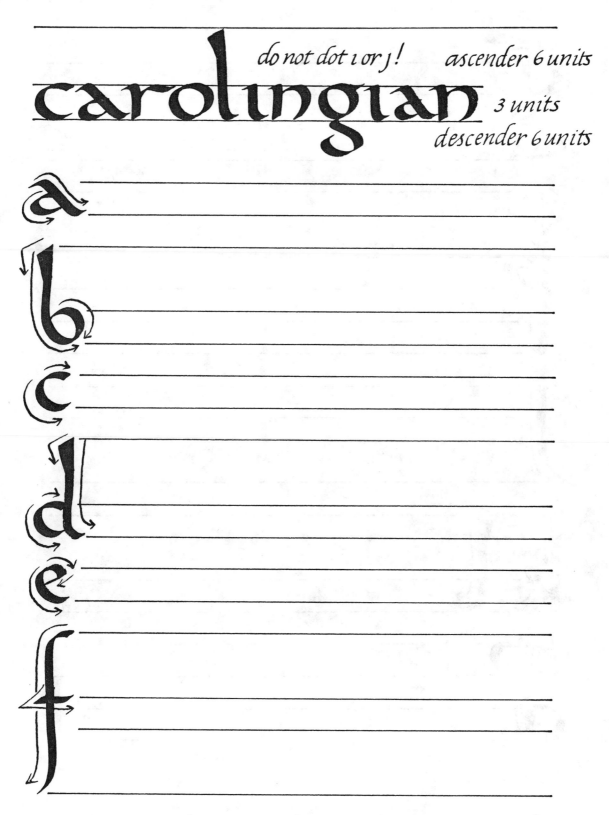

carolingian

do not dot ı or ȷ! *ascender 6 units*

3 units

descender 6 units

a

b

c

d

e

f

Write these with care · Double-stroke ascender serifs.

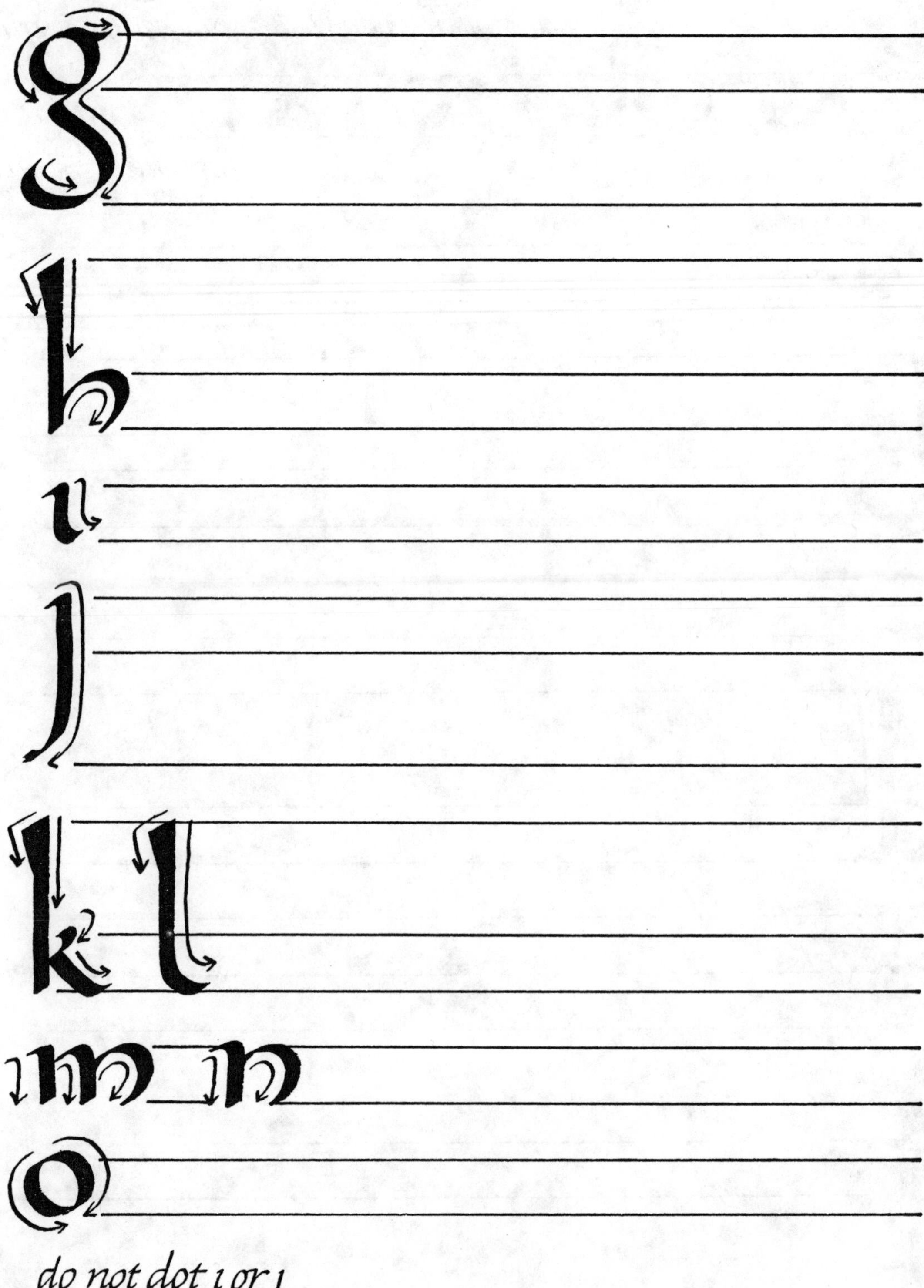

do not dot ı or ȷ

Use Versals or Uncials for emphasis. Can also be on a slight angle, when written. abcdefgh etc

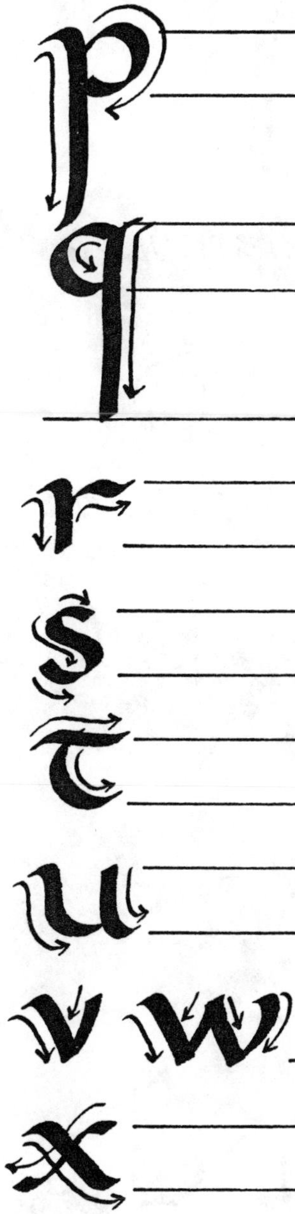

p

q

r

s

t

u

v w

x

z

y

raise upon
left edge of
pen - right side is off paper.

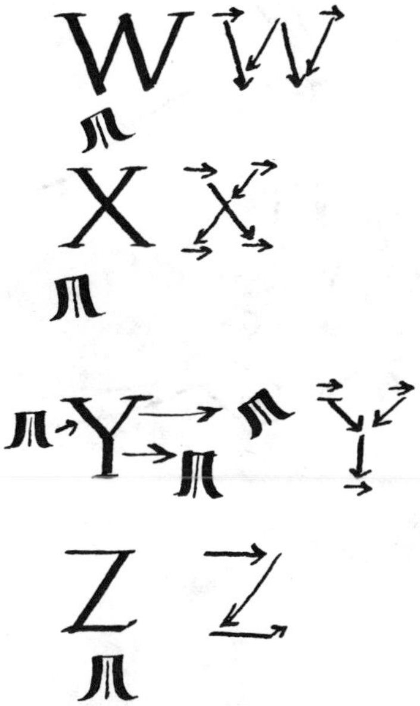

W W

X X

Y Y

Z Z

abcdefghijkl
mnopqrstu
vwxyz

Use wide ruled notebook paper to practice writing these.

The masters wrote with the Quill and modern scribes still use them for their finest work. Quill pens are fun to use, and a challenge to make.

QUILLS

Edward Johnston said *"The main advantages of a quill over a metal pen are that the former may be "sharpened or "shaped exactly as the writer desires, and be re-cut when it becomes blunt."*

Alfred Fairbank wrote *"The blunt quills may have been worn but possibly on occasion were cut so as to be blunt and more easily running, for sharply cut quills tend to kick and splutter when pushed against the edge."*

Benson & Carey said *"Turkey quills tend to bend when drying, so cut the nib short with a final split of less than 1/8 of an inch, as the points may otherwise separate after it has been wet in ink. Avoid turkey quills if you can."*

William Bishop wrote *"In its natural state, the barrel or quill has a greasy external skin or membrane, and an internal pith, and is inclined to be soft. To remedy this, it must first be dressed or cured, by hardening the quill and removing the fatty surface and internal pith."*

Abraham Lincoln said *"I wouldn't own one unless it is the complete wing feather; and about twelve inches long, from a mature goose, or possibly from a swan. Zoos are about the only place you can get these, and usually, once or twice a year."*

QUILLS

The evidence is clear that the monks and writing masters wrote with their quills upon an inclined writing surface. The angle was often as steep as 60 degrees; and such an angle allowed a penman to control the ink flowing from his quill.

ROXIME
Psalteriuz quo
strictis & nece...
annotatum in cõn
uterq; depræhẽdin
perstrinxisse leuiter
liquisse: de quibus
disputauit: quo scil
gnam breui sermo
pro familiaritate q
se & sedule postula
gna memoria uide
dam potius quã i
notarem. Et (quod
breui tabella terrarum & urbium situs pingunt: &
modico spatio conantur ostendere) ita in psalteri
præteriẽs aliqua perstringerẽ: ut ex paucis quæ te
& cætera quæ ommissa sunt: quam uim habeant a
putem a me posse dici quæ ille præterit: sed quo
homeliis ipse disseruit uel ego digna arbitror lect.

from the print shop of Geovanni and Gregorio de Gregoriis, Venice, 1498

Edward Johnston wrote "*The slope of the desk may be about, or rather less than 45° to begin with: as the hand becomes accustomed to it, it may be raised to about 60°.*"

Alfred Fairbank gives us another reason for a raised surface "*The professional calligrapher works at a slope of say 45°, sitting up comfortably and seeing his work truly. The steep slope allows the direction of his sight to be at right angles to the writing-surface without his bending forward.*"

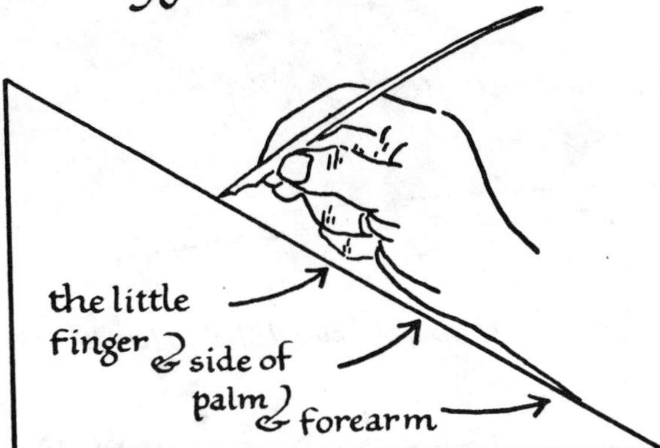

the inclined surface shown here is only 30°.

William M. Aaron said "*The small finger and inner side of palm of the right hand and elbow muscle rest on the desk or writing board. This position allows the hand and forearm to perform the functions of writing with comparative ease.*"

Obviously, there are several reasons for the steep writing-surface and one is for ink flow.

A professional calligrapher must control the flow of ink from his pen or quill. See illustration below.

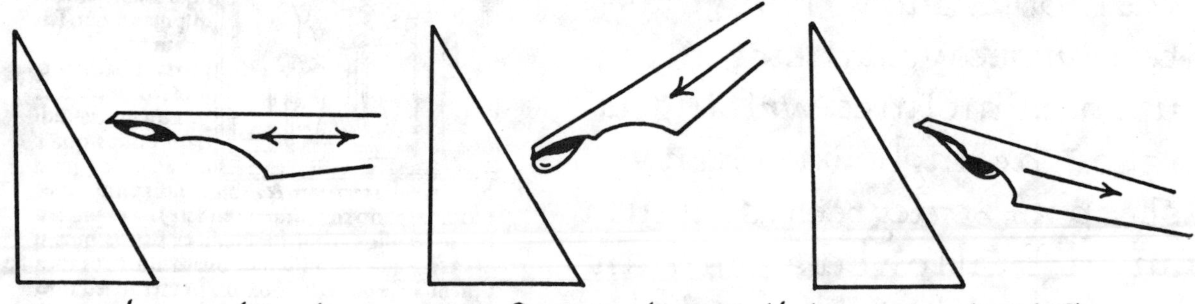

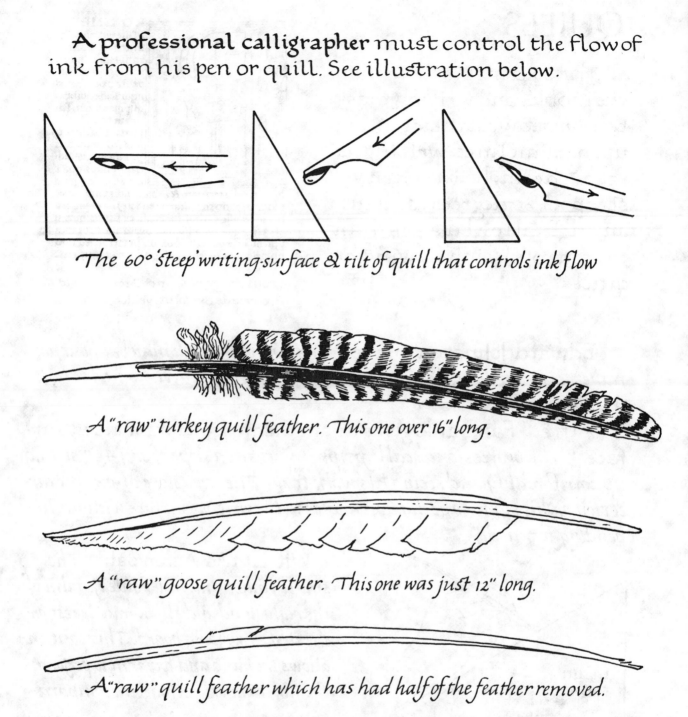

The 60° 'steep' writing-surface & tilt of quill that controls ink flow

A "raw" turkey quill feather. This one over 16" long.

A "raw" goose quill feather. This one was just 12" long.

A "raw" quill feather which has had half of the feather removed.

The selected feather should be free of splits and excessive warps. The old masters have said that the raw quill must be free of grease; the pith removed and then hardened. First, they recommended heating the quill in hot ashes and then to carefully scrape the barrel of the quill with the back of a blade to remove the external membrane. Then the barrel is further cleaned and polished with a piece of woolen cloth or even fish skin. A seventeenth century method suggests that the outer membrane be scraped off, and that both ends of the quill be cut off. After this they were put into boiling water. The water also contained a small amount of salt and alum. After 15 minutes, the quills were dried either in an oven or in a tray of hot sand.

Robert Hostetter says "*A teaspoon of alum to a cup of water. Heat is then applied by slowly rolling the end of quill on the smooth face of an electric iron heated to the temperature used for pressing rayon.*"

quoted from Quill Cutting by R. Hostetter

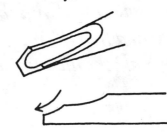

A very sharp knife cuts off the end prior to boiling

side view

Make this your second cut

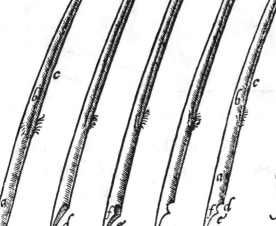

c c d e g b g b f d e

Make this your third cut

The example at left is by Arrighi and is from Three Classics of Italian Calligraphy · Ogg · Dover Publications · N.Y.C.

A slight "nick" or cut is made in the tip of the nib. This will be split in the next step.

Use the small round handle of an artist's brush, or similar round object to push into the quill.

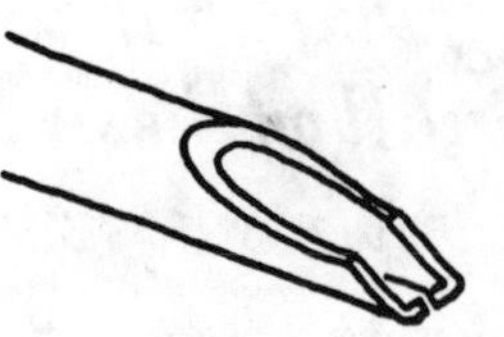

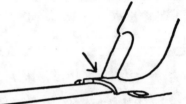

With the thumbnail pressed firmly against the quill and ab't 3/16" from the tip of nib, raise-up the end of the brush. The nib will split from the 'nick' up to where your thumbnail is pressed.

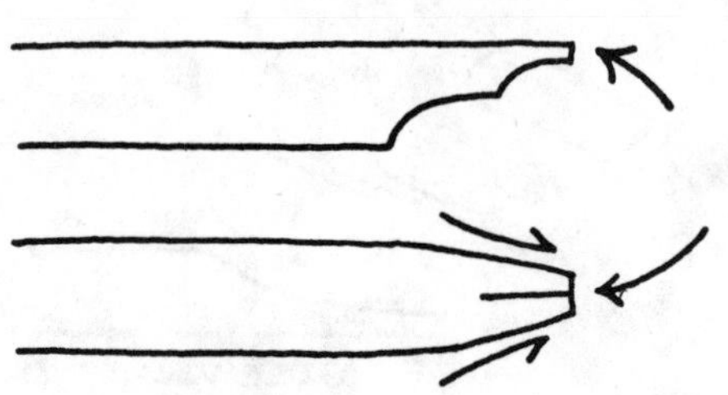

At this stage the nib is still cut square and must be beveled; and the sides may be cut to make the nib smaller.

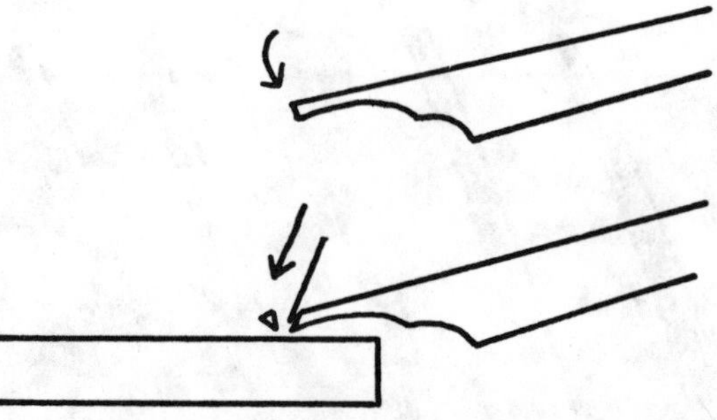

This is the last cut, made on the quill, and is made with a sharp knife as the quill is held on a hard surface, such as glass.

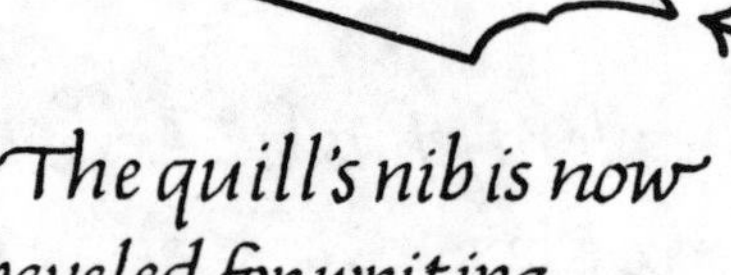

The quill's nib is now beveled for writing.

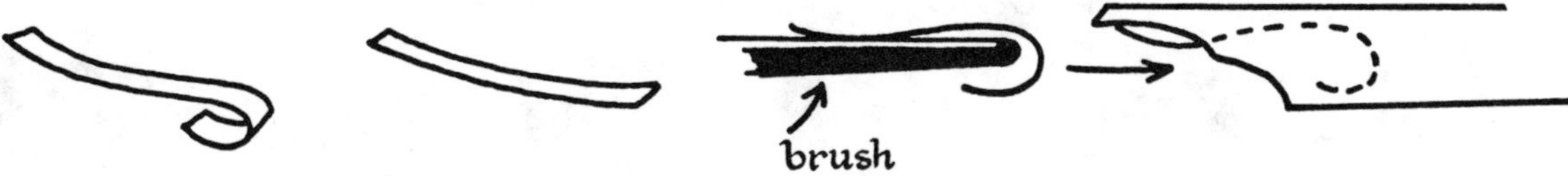

A thin strip of metal can be cut from a beer can or soft drink can with scissors, and curved as shown. This will be an ink reservoir.

The ink reservoir can be pushed into the quill with the 'round brush handle. The reservoir will hold the ink while you write and you don't dip as often.

Three things bear mighty Sway with Men,
The Sword, the Scepter, and the PEN;
Who can the least of these Command,
In the First Rank of Fame will Stand.

Joseph Champion · 1740's

If you want, raw turkey quills can be purchased from Calligrafree ...

the References quoted

Writing & Illuminating & Lettering by Edward Johnston · Pitman Publishing Corp. pages 26 · 28 ~1969
A Handwriting Manual by Alfred Fairbank · Watson-Guptill Publications · N.Y.C. pages 38 · 30 ~1975
The Elements of Lettering by Benson & Carey · McGraw-Hill Book Company, Inc. N.Y. pages 44 ~1950
The Calligrapher's Handbook edited by C.M. Lamb · Faber & Faber Limited · London pages 34 ~1968
Italic Writing · A concise guide by W.M. Aaron · London/Alec Tiranti pages 12 ~1971

Sheet can be used for any style in workbook

This is an assignment sheet and should be used to make up a "poor" assignment; or, a self improvement sheet, for the weakest letters in your notebook.

a few things to look for.

strive to make the "counter" the same in all similar letters. agedq bp

h keep this triangular area open & equal nmruy

s s s s s s try this technique on s

v v w v w similar shapes

k e the bowls, or counters, are not exactly alike.

a g the tops are flat on all similar letters.

x cross just above center

ta t is "just" taller

Pens and Ink Recommended by the Author

It is nice to purchase a new book. Many people are really excited about using a new book for the first time. And, it is equally exciting to purchase new tools for use in the new book. There are a number of pens and pen sets which are now available for use in calligraphy. Some of these are much better than others, and the new style Osmiroid pens are among the best pens and sets available in this country. I really think the new Osmiroid Master Calligraphy Set is ideal for use in this book. I certainly recommend it to you. I would caution you to purchase one B3 nib extra, and possibly one B6 nib extra. If you also purchase an extra barrel and cap assembly then you will not have to change nibs as often.

You can also buy ink cartridges to use in your pen, or I would recommend that you consider Osmiroid Free Flowing Black Ink. Be sure that you take the time to flush your pen out with clean water, from time to time. A clean pen writes much better than a dirty one.

You can use the Speedball "C" style dip pens on lessons in this book. Since beginners usually have more than enough problems learning about calligraphy, I would recommend the purchase of the fountain pen set described above. If you are left handed, you can buy left handed fountain pens or Speedball "C" style dip pens. Turn to page 5 in this book to see the difference between left and right hand pens.

Abraham Lincoln
September 1982

LETTERING AND DRAWING PENS, HOLDERS AND STEEL BRUSHES

HUNTSPEEDBALL

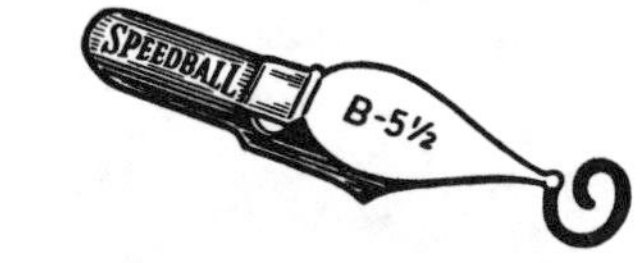

SPEEDBALL LETTERING & DRAWING PENS

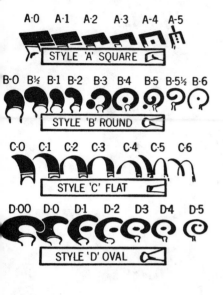

A-0 A-1 A-2 A-3 A-4 A-5

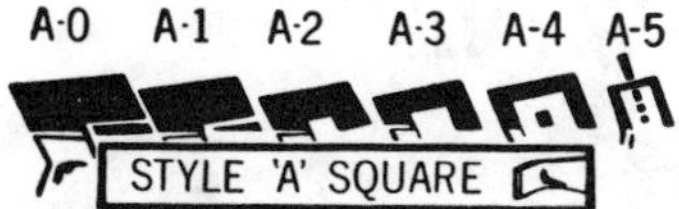

B-0 B½ B-1 B-2 B-3 B-4 B-5 B-5½ B-6

STYLE 'B' ROUND

C-0 C-1 C-2 C-3 C-4 C-5 C-6

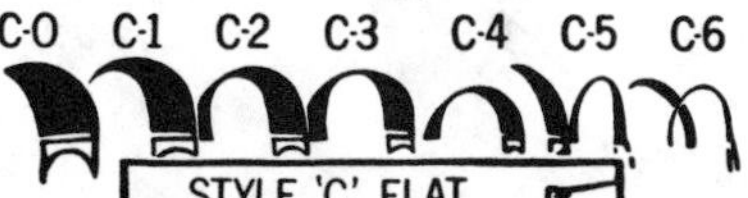

D-00 D-0 D-1 D-2 D-3 D-4 D-5

PEN HOLDER

o. 9451. Packed one dozen per box, weight oz. For all types of SPEEDBALL Pens and Steel rushes.

PEEDBALL PEN KIT NO. 1

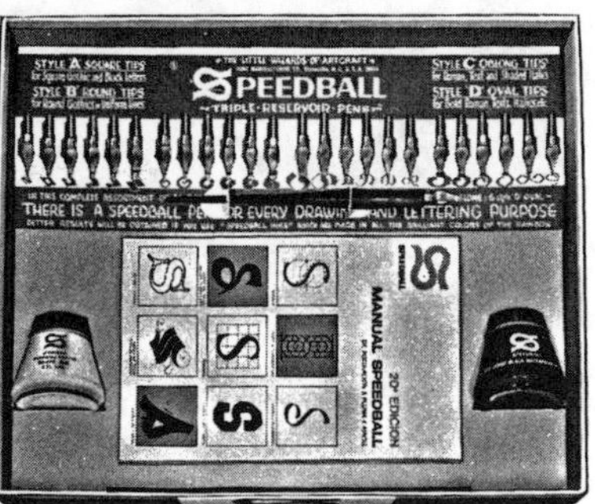

Assorted SPEEDBALL Pens in A, B, C, D yles. One jar each 2 oz. Black and White Ink. ne Penholder. 96-page SPEEDBALL Lettering ook. Individually gift boxed.

SPEEDBALL FLICKER® LETTERING PENS

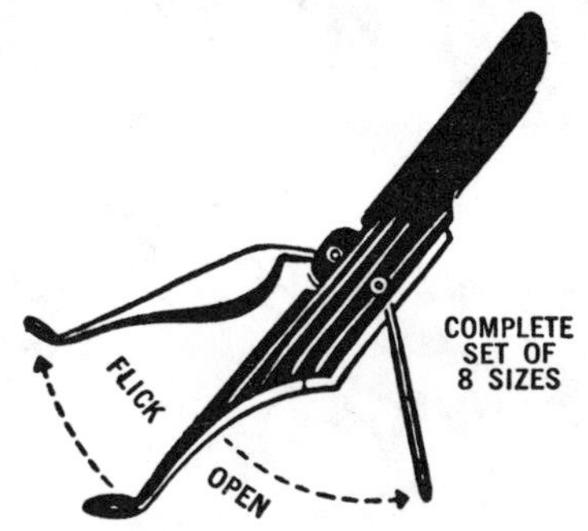

FLICKER Pens are similar to standard SPEEDBALL Lettering Pens but are equipped with an adjustable gold-plated reservoir that may be opened for pen cleaning.

SPEEDBALL STEEL BRUSH

As interchangeable as a pen point, four sizes. As easy to use as a conventional brush or pen. For charts, lettering, illustrations. Each SPEEDBALL Steel Brush individually packed in a deluxe plastic case.

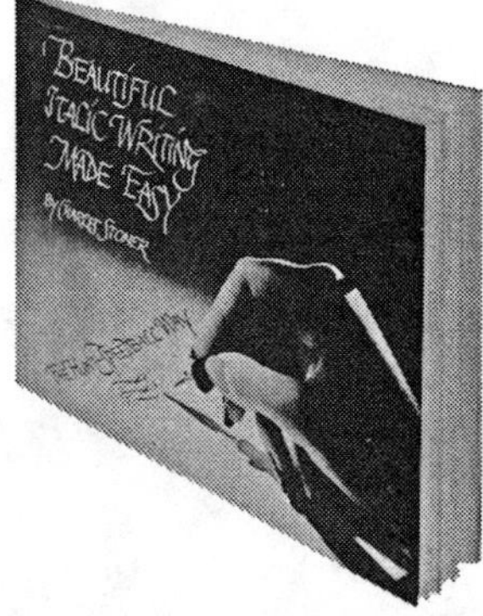

THE NEWEST INSTRUCTION BOOK FROM HUNT SPEEDBALL

"Beautiful Italic Writing Made Easy" by Charles Stoner. Easy to learn writing techniques, fully illustrated and simple-to-follow instructions.

FAMOUS SPEEDBALL TEXTBOOK, 20th Edition

This "best seller" among lettering books is a practical 96-page manual on all lettering and poster forms. An excellent reference book. Color section. Edited by Ross F. George. No. 3067.

SPEEDBALL ELEMENTARY ALPHABET BOOK

24-page book covering the basic alphabets, drafting alphabet, and manuscript. By Ross F. George

CALLIGRAPHIC PAPERS

Fine quality Parchment with a high degree of clarity. Ideal for award certificates, diplomas and personalized greeting cards.

A final word ...

This book was written by hand by the author.

All of the author's work is shown full size and was not retouched. Any errors in this edition are not intentional and any omis-sions are regrettable.

An Osmiroid fountain pen with a B-3 nib is suggested for use in the workbook. The Osmiroid Lettering Set is useful and will give you a complete range of nibs. The C-3 Speedball pen with holder can also be used on many assignments in the workbook.

A comprehensive set of Teacher's Lesson Plans is available for use with this workbook, at additional cost.

A.L.

Italic B-3

Osmiroid nib

Italic Broad

Osmiroid nib

Italic Fine *Osmiroid nib*

Italic Extra Fine

Osmiroid nib

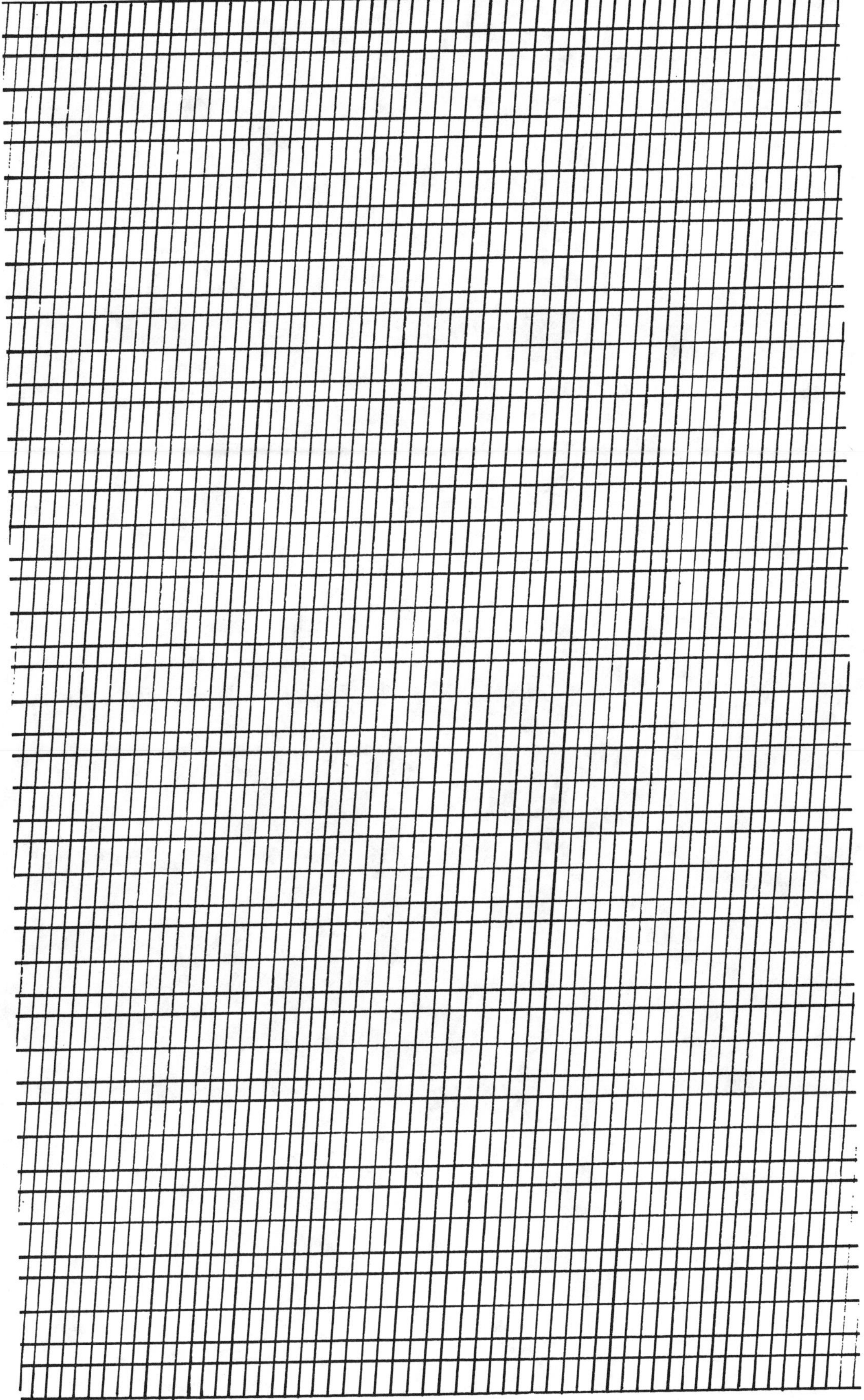

Fine or Extra Fine ✣ With Letter Slant Guide Lines · Italic